ENGLISH INFLUENCES
on
VINCENT VAN GOGH

100   van Gogh   THE STATE LOTTERY   (F970) Watercolour and bodycolour

An exhibition organised by
the Fine Art Department,
University of Nottingham and
the Arts Council of Great Britain
1974/5

copyright © Ronald Pickvance   Introduction and
catalogue
Catalogue designed by Bridget Heal
Printed by Balding and Mansell Ltd
ISBN 0 7287 0027 1

A list of Arts Council publications, including all exhibition catalogues in print, can be obtained from the Publications Department, Arts Council of Great Britain, 105
Piccadilly, London W1V 0AU.

PREFACE

This exhibition in one sense is the centenary celebration of Vincent van Gogh's stay in England (1873–76). Its aims are to recount something of the effects of this – on his life, his appreciation of English literature and, not least, his art. It also gives an airing to an unjustly forgotten group of English illustrators.

The idea for the exhibition was suggested by Ronald Pickvance, Senior Lecturer in the History of Art, University of Nottingham. The Arts Council welcomed the opportunity of sharing the organization of the exhibition with the University of Nottingham. Without the willing cooperation of Dr V W van Gogh, Chairman of the Vincent van Gogh Foundation, Amsterdam, and Dr E R Meijer, Director of the Rijksmuseum Vincent van Gogh, it would not have been possible. As on previous occasions in 1948, 1955 and 1968, the Arts Council is very much in Dr van Gogh's debt. We are delighted to be able to reprint in this catalogue his essay on *The Sources of Inspiration of Vincent van Gogh*. We are further grateful to Dr van Gogh and Dr Meijer for kindly allowing the exhibition to visit seven other galleries in England after the Nottingham showing.

We add our thanks to the New York Graphic Society for allowing us to quote from their edition of *The Complete Letters of Vincent van Gogh* (1958), and to the Trustees of the Tate Gallery and National Gallery, and to the directors of the Victoria and Albert Museum and the Rijksmuseum Kröller-Müller for permission to reproduce works in their collections. The editor of the *Illustrated London News* kindly allowed reproduction of many of the illustrations.

Professor Alastair Smart
Department of Fine Art
University of Nottingham

Norbert Lynton
Director of Exhibitions
Arts Council of Great Britain

ACKNOWLEDGEMENTS

First, I should like to express my profound debt of gratitude to Dr V W van Gogh and Dr E R Meijer without whose enthusiasm and generosity this exhibition would not have been possible. Their colleagues at the Rijksmuseum Vincent van Gogh in Amsterdam have been of inestimable help. I should like particularly to thank Mrs Lili Couvée-Jampoller and Mr Han van Crimpen. I have benefited, over several years, from many fruitful discussions on van Gogh with Mrs Annet Tellegen-Hoogendoorn of the Netherlands Institute for Art History in The Hague. I have received many kindnesses from Dr Ellen Joosten at the Kröller-Müller Museum, Otterlo.

The staff of the Fine Art Department of the University of Nottingham have coped devotedly with a variety of requests and problems. One of my former students, Mr D G Lee, took the trouble to trace some material on obscure and forgotten artists. I am most grateful to David Jones for his unstinting professionalism with the tasks of photography. Reference librarians at Chiswick, Hounslow, Lewisham, Nottingham, Richmond and the Guildhall libraries have been extremely helpful in the unearthing of documentary and photographic material. A special word of thanks is due to Mr C E Busson, librarian of Ramsgate Public Library, for help with van Gogh in Ramsgate. Mr Leo Garvin and Mr E T Reid provided some information on, and photographs of, Holme Court, Isleworth. I am most grateful to Mr John Sunderland and his staff of the Witt Library for help with photographs, especially those of Goupil et Cie. Professor Philip Collins has kindly helped to solve some puzzles about Dickens. Bridget Heal has devoted much care to the design of the catalogue. For her constant support and encouragement through many an illustrated page, I owe a special debt of gratitude to my wife.

Ronald Pickvance
Senior Lecturer in the History of Art
University of Nottingham.

VAN GOGH'S SOURCES OF INSPIRATION

When he was an employee of Goupil in London (1873–75) Vincent was already interested in wood-engravings. In a letter to his painter-friend van Rappard (R 20, beginning of February 1883) he writes:

> I assure you that the *Graphics* I have now are amazingly interesting. More than ten years ago I was in London, I used to go every week to the show windows of the printing offices of the *Graphic* and the *London News* to see the new issues. The impressions I got on the spot were so strong that, notwithstanding all that has happened to me since, the drawings are clear in my mind. . . . at least my enthusiasm for those things is rather stronger than it was even then.

At the time photography was not yet in use to illustrate articles. For the illustration of a text one needed to dispose of drawings. From the drawing a wood-engraving was made by another person, generally of the size of a whole magazine page. This was the origin of a generation of draughtsmen and wood-engravers. The subject of the illustrations is still the same to-day: when an event had to be illustrated, a draughtsman was sent to do the reporting, even in case of travel reports in remote countries. Vincent admired these draughtsmen with good reason. Having become a professional painter and living in Nuenen (Holland) with his parents, he would buy bound volumes of English illustrated reviews. He would cut out the beautiful engravings and mount them by the hundreds on dark greyish-brown paper of the size of 30 × 40 cm. Engravings of *L'Illustration* were often taken again by English reviews and vice versa. Exchanges also took place between the English and the Americans.

Living in the Hague, Vincent writes to Theo (LT 183, Friday 24 March, 1882):

> Blommers (Dutch painter) spoke to me about showing a collection of wood engravings after Herkomer, Frank Holl, du Maurier, etc, some evening at Pulchri (the exhibition-hall of the association of the painters of the Hague) I should like very much to do so. I have enough of them for at least two evenings.

And a few days later (LT 184, beginning of April 1882):

> Blommers came to see me about the exhibition of wood engravings. He looked at them for three hours and was angry at the committee of Pulchri for saying something like, 'Those things one sees now and then in the South Holland café' (the name of a big coffee house of the Hague where one could read the papers at a large table). If that's all they know about wood engravings, they are indeed competent to judge them! . . . But Blommers wants to have his way, . . . It is very curious to hear some painters talk about what they call 'illustrators', about Gavarni, for instance, or Herkomer. Not knowing anything about the matter is what makes up part of their so-called general information. Much good may it do them.

The engravings kept by Vincent are in the first place representations of groups of persons, in the street, at meetings of all kinds, which occupied the minds of those days. There are scenes of the siege of Paris and of the Commune, scenes of charity, the crowd in the streets, etc.

In Vincent's work of the period of the Hague there are subjects recalling this kind of representations (the watercolour of the 'Lottery', the 'Distribution of Food'). In Nuenen there is particularly the 'Sale of the Crosses' of the old cemetery, and the 'Timber Auction'. Among the wood-engravings one also finds other subjects. There is a whole series of beautiful portraits of famous persons, statesmen, writers, etc. Numerous images concern men and women at work, especially in the fields, but also weavers of which Vincent has made several paintings and drawings.

Lastly there are reproductions of well-known paintings of Rembrandt, J-F Millet and others, as well as reproductions of engravings of Gustave Doré, Daumier, Gavarni, etc. Later on they will serve Vincent for his own compositions (see further on).

During his first period in Paris, from May 1875 to March 1876, Vincent – he was 22 – takes a great interest in engravings and reproductions of all kinds. The art firm Goupil, where he was employed, not only dealt in paintings, but also published reproductions, especially of lithographs and of wood-engravings. He writes to Theo that he has rented a small room in Montmartre (LT 30, July 6, 1875) the walls of which he has decorated with reproductions. At that time he composes a book of images in which figures the same artists, like Théodore Rousseau, Daubigny, Jules Dupré, Corot. There is "a beautiful Jacque, a melancholy landscape with sheep." (LT 49, December 13, 1875) which will serve him later in The Hague to make a painting. After Nuenen, Vincent's interest for reviews keeps showing and in the beginning in Paris he mounts the engravings on grey paper as before. In course of time he can't manage this any longer, but he collects nevertheless numerous sheets with reproductions of Forain, Willette, of the *Charivari* with Daumier, etc.

At the beginning of his activities as a professional painter, Vincent starts to study the human figure by copying the drawings of the *Cours de Dessin, Exercices au Fusain* by Ch Bargue, an important publication of the art firm Goupil. He copied about sixty of them three times (LT 134, Cuesmes 20 August 1880). He continued to make these copies in Paris.

During his stay in Paris Vincent discovers the Japanese prints, something new. He made a whole collection of them. As he did not have the money to buy the famous masters, he chose about 200 small artists.

He keeps also, among others, complete numbers of *La Vie Populaire* and of *Le Courrier Français*. In those reviews authors, now well-known, published their great works or some short stories: Emile Zola, Guy de Maupassant, les Goncourts, etc. Often their wood-engraved portrait accompanied the text. Vincent also gathered art criticisms of all kinds.

Theo possessed numerous books about the artists: about Rembrandt, Millet, etc. He also had the catalogue of etchings and wood-engravings, of lithographs and photographs, published by the art firm Goupil.

About the literary authors Vincent writes: (W 1, summer of autumn 1887)

> If on the contrary one wants truth, life as it is, then there are for instance de Goncourt in *Germinie Lacerteux, la Fille Elisa*, Zola in *La joie de vivre* and *L'assommoir* and so many other masterpieces; they paint life as they feel it themselves, and thus they satisfy the need we all feel of being told the truth.
> The work of the French naturalists, Zola, Flaubert, Guy de Maupassant, de Goncourt, Richepin, Daudet, Huysmans, is magnificent, and one can hardly be said to belong to one's time if one has paid no attention to it.

In the still life representing the large Bible of his father he added *La Joie de vivre* by Emile Zola. He painted two paintings entitled 'Romans Parisiens' (or 'Parisian Novels') and another one representing a little statue and two books, *Bel Ami* by Guy de Maupassant and *Germinie Lacerteux* by Jules and Edmond de Goncourt. Many books read by Vincent are still there; in two of them he wrote his name (*Chérie* by the brothers Goncourt and *L'Amour* by Michelet). At the time the yellow or green paper covers were regular. About 1900, some titles were replaced by copies in a better state, and the set has been bound.

The whole of the documentation reveals that outside the exhibitions at Theo's gallery of Degas, Pissarro, Raffaelli, Monet, the two brothers van Gogh were conversant with the vanguard art of their time.

In the South of France (Arles and Saint-Rémy) there are moments Vincent does not go out, but keeps on working. To divert him Theo sends him reproductions and photographs of famous paintings. There are among others proofs of small reproductions from the 'Travaux des champs' of Millet, meant for a book coming out.

It is then that Vincent writes to Theo (LT 607, St Rémy, about 20 September 1889):

> You will be surprised at the effect 'Les Travaux des Champs' takes on in colour, it is a very profound series of his. I am going to try to tell you what I am seeking in it and why it seems good to me to copy them. We painters are always asked to compose ourselves and be nothing but composers. So be it – but it isn't like that in music – and if some person or other plays Beethoven, he adds his personal interpretation – in music and more especially in singing – the interpretation of a composer is something, and it is not a hard and fast rule that only the composer should play his own composition.
>
> Very good and I, mostly because I am ill at present, I am trying to do something to console myself, for my own pleasure.
>
> I let the black and white by Delacroix or Millet or something made after their work pose for me as a subject. And then I improvise colour on it, not, you understand, altogether myself, but searching for memories of their pictures –but the memory, 'the vague consonance of colours which are at least right in feeling' – that is my own interpretation. Many people do not copy, many others do – I started on it accidentally, and I find that it teaches me things, and above all it sometimes gives me consolation.

This quotation justifies and illuminates the exhibition of the sources of inspiration of van Gogh.

It is rather a miracle that the whole of the documentation has been kept, in the first place thanks to Mrs J van Gogh-Bonger, Theo's wife, my mother.

Dr V W van Gogh

This essay is translated from the French introduction to the catalogue of the exhibition, *les Sources d'inspiration de Vincent van Gogh*, which was held at the Institut Néerlandais, Paris, in January-March 1972.

INTRODUCTION

You will probably think the interior of the empty bedroom with a wooden bedstead and two chairs the most unbeautiful thing of all – and notwithstanding this I have painted it twice, on a large scale. I wanted to achieve an effect of simplicity of the sort one finds described in *Felix Holt*. After being told this you may quickly understand this picture, but it will probably remain ridiculous in the eyes of others who have not been warned. (Letter to his sister Wil, 30 April 1889)

The figure in the Scottish plaid with orange and green checks stands out against the sombre green of the cypress, which contrast is further accentuated by the red parasol – this figure gives me an impression of you like those in Dickens's novels, a vaguely representative figure. (Letter to his sister Wil, late November 1888)

I have been re-reading Dickens's Christmas books these days. There are things in them so profound that one must read them over and over again, there's a tremendously close connection with Carlyle. (Letter to Theo, early April 1889)

Vincent van Gogh is the one major Post-Impressionist whose being was seeped in English literature; the one who broke the narrow, chauvinistic, self-regarding barriers of French art of the 1880's; the one who, having lived in England for almost three years, having experienced the idiosyncrasies of its capital, its people, its painters, its illustrators and its novelists, was most prone to re-assert those memories from his complex and multi-experienced consciousness. So they surface in unexpected places: in such quintessentially Post-Impressionist images as his 'Bedroom', where George Eliot's *Felix Holt* evidently supplies the clue to its meaning; and the 'Memory of the Garden at Etten' where his sister takes on the role of a representative Dickens figure, a kind of Rosa Bud with parasol – and unlikely Scottish plaid. And if *Edwin Drood* as illustrated by Luke Fildes supplies a possible source for his representative Dickens figure (and he was as much at home with the illustrators of Dickens as he was with the novels themselves), then another Fildes illustration could perhaps suggest subconscious analogies with the 'Bedroom'. Notice that he calls it the *empty bedroom*, the only occasion he refers to it as such. One thinks of Fildes' 'Empty Chair', that monumental *nature morte* that Vincent had once so greatly admired. And the chair in Fildes' last illustration to *Edwin Drood* suddenly becomes a candidate for discussion in the election of prototypes for 'Gauguin's Chair'. (cf p 24). Yet another image that he held in great esteem in The Hague was Fred Walker's 'Harbour of Refuge' (p 73): what small contribution might that have made to the imaginative genesis of the 'Memory of the Garden at Etten'? More tangibly, Dickens' *Christmas Books* (with Beecher Stowe's *Uncle Tom's Cabin*) physically exist on the table in 'L'Arlésienne' (p 38), yet are spiritual tokens and talismen. And who but Vincent would make that enigmatic connexion with Carlyle, he who knew his Carlyle almost as well as his Dickens? Further pictorial analogies can be notched up. They may appear far-fetched, absurd and irrelevant. Take the portrait of Patience Escalier: peasant of the Crau, painted in the full majestic mastery of his Arles palette, yet, for Vincent himself, recalling his peasants of Nuenen – and through them, one might add, the 'Heads of the People' that he had once so admired in the *Graphic*. Or take the heads of Roulin the postman, or Milliet the soldier, or even of Boch the poet: have the 'Heads of the People' still retained a spectral existence? Then think of the 'Night Café', with its vestiges of Herkomer's 'Schuhplattl Dance', or its atmosphere of a sailors' assembly room of the Ratcliffe Highway, where truly in the London of the 1870's "the café is a place where one can ruin oneself."

He read Dickens and Beecher Stowe in the Borinage

in 1879; he re-read them in Arles ten years later. He also read Shakespeare in the Borinage in 1879; he read him again in St. Rémy in 1889. The hold of English literature persists. So does the English language. English titles are given to several of his early drawings: 'Sorrow', 'Bearers of the Burden', 'The Great Lady', 'Worn Out', 'At Eternity's Gate'. He often quotes English proverbs. He is still able to write a postcard in English to Theo from The Hague in 1882 (cf p 12); later in Paris he can write a long letter in English to an artist friend; and as late as 1890 he can still handle the language in a letter to another artist-friend, John Russell. He will often quote a passage from Dickens, or Eliot, or Carlyle in his letters; yet, oddly enough, only once does he appear to have set out to illustrate an English text – that of Thomas Hood in *The Great Lady* (p 26).

He could write of English pictures that "with a few exceptions they are very bad and uninteresting." (LT 11). Yet he could write of English Black-and-White illustration: "There is something virile in it – something rugged – which attracts me strongly." (R 20). How much in fact did he know of English painting? And why at one stage of his life did he collect so avidly the *Graphic* and the *Illustrated London News*? How important was the English influence? These are some of the questions that this exhibition tries to answer. It concentrates on certain aspects and one or two representative figures. It can't aim at comprehensiveness: that would mean a much larger exhibition, more illustrations and a longer introduction. First, it will look at the experiences of Vincent's stay in England between 1873 and 1876; secondly, it will glance at his views on English painting (to do this properly, the whole of contemporary European art, much of which Vincent was familiar with, should be considered); thirdly, it will concentrate on Dickens and George Eliot to the exclusion of Carlyle, the Brontës, Bulwer Lytton, Thomas Hood, Keats, Shakespeare and others; fourthly, it will look at the *Graphic* and the *Illustrated London News*, and exclude *Punch* (of which a large selection still exists in Amsterdam, especially of Sambourne), the *British Workman*, the *Pictorial News* and other British periodicals he is known to have collected, and exclude too any reasonable discussion of the many French magazines he collected. Finally, it will look at his work in The Hague only as reflecting the English influence and will therefore ignore, through lack of examples and of space, the Nuenen period and beyond; and even in The Hague period, during which he relived his London experiences and lived out his awareness of English novels and of English Black-and-White artists, only selected aspects will be presented. In short, this exhibition is an appetiser, a small progress report on a fairly large and somewhat neglected subject. And generous though the number of illustrations may appear to be, they are but a fraction of those he knew.

SOME NOTES ON VINCENT IN ENGLAND

1 The loss of Vincent's letters to his parents severely reduces our knowledge of his first stay in London (May 1873 to May 1875). Had he prepared himself with guidebook and novel? What were his first impressions of England before he arrived in London itself? His letters to Theo were infrequent at this stage, often with a gap of two months. And he was in London for more than three weeks before he sent his first letter to his brother (13 June). Some measure of the differences between his letters to his parents and those to Theo can be gauged by comparing the first surviving letter to his parents from Ramsgate (LT 60) with that to Theo (LT 61), written on the same

7

day: the one is lengthy, descriptive and often detailed, the other is brief and telegraphic.

However, in the letters that do survive, his descriptions of Rotten Row, of the beautiful parks in London, and of the suburban houses with small gardens of flowers and a few trees at the front are not just the overawed reactions of a simple, wide-eyed country boy. It is worth remembering that he knew The Hague extremely well; he was well acquainted with Amsterdam; he had visited "beautiful pleasant Brussels" (eg for the Belgian Salon in the summer of 1872), and had spent several days in Paris in May 1873 before his arrival in London. Moreover, Vincent's reactions to the London scene are not unlike those expressed in Jerrold's text to Doré's *London*. "London under green leaves presents, in short, to the foreigner, a constant source of wonder and delight. Then, again, the suburbs of London are renowned, wherever travelled people abide, for their rich and rare natural beauties." (p 102). Vincent doesn't mention Doré until after he had finally left England. Yet an important volume like *London* by Europe's best-known illustrator, published in 1872, must surely have been known to him. Equally, he doesn't mention Dickens until November 1876: a reference that makes it clear that he had read Dickens in Holland. These are examples of the frequently unrevelatory nature of his letters from England.

2 *Goupil*

Vincent had spent almost four years in The Hague, conscientiously learning the profession of art dealer in the firm of Goupil. He was sent to London at the instigation of his uncle Vincent. Was it just to improve his English and to widen his experience? "In London, Goupil has no gallery, but sells only directly to art dealers," he wrote to Theo in March 1873 (LT5). And on 13 June, he explained, "I am not so busy here as I was in The Hague; I work only from nine until six, and on Saturdays we close at four o'clock." (LT9). Nonetheless, it would seem from the evidence of the stockbooks of The Hague branch of Goupil that Vincent's transfer to London was part of a newly launched policy. That policy was to expand the London business from just a photograph and print-selling wholesale house to one where paintings would be increasingly handled and where ultimately an exhibition gallery would be opened. The Hague stockbooks reveal that the first batch of paintings and watercolours was sent to London on 28 June 1873, that is to say a month after Vincent's arrival; that a further batch was sent in December 1873, and others followed at regular intervals. Vincent himself reflects this expansionist policy in a letter of 19 November 1873 (LT12): "Lately we have had many pictures and drawings here; we sold a great many, but not enough yet – it must become something more established and solid. I think there is still much work to do in England, but it will not be successful at once. Of course, the first thing necessary is to have good pictures, and that will be very difficult." He continues: "Here the ordinary engravings after Brochart do not sell at all, the good burin engravings sell pretty well. From the 'Venus Anadyomene' after Ingres we have already sold twenty *épreuves d'artiste*. It is a pleasure to see how well the photographs sell, especially the coloured ones, and there is a big profit in them. We sell the Musée Goupil & Co photographs only *en papillottes*, on an average of a hundred a day."

Subsequently, Vincent tells of having paintings by Apol, Jacquet and Boldini – and even of selling one by Matthew Maris. The new policy began to pay dividends. In July 1874, Vincent confides to Theo (LT20): "Probably we are going to move on 1 January 1875, to another, larger shop. Mr Obach is in Paris just now to decide whether we shall take over that other business or not. Don't speak about it to anybody for the moment." And while Vincent himself – much against his will – was temporarily transferred to Paris from October to December 1874, the "larger shop" was taken over. The *Athenaeum* of 21 November 1874 announced: "We understand that the business of Messrs Holloway & Son, print-sellers, will, in future, be carried on by MM Goupil, of London, Paris, Amsterdam, and The Hague. MM Goupil retain the staff and all the business relations of Messrs Holloway & Son."

By the time Vincent returned to London in January 1875, preparations were afoot. He reported to Theo in February (LT22): "Our gallery is ready now and is very beautiful, we have some splendid pictures: Jules Dupré, Michel, Daubigny, Israëls, Mauve, Bisschop, etc. In April we are going to have an exhibition. Mr Boussod has promised to send us the best things available: 'La Malaria' by Hébert, 'La Falaise' by Jules Breton, etc." As it turned out, the first exhibition was not opened in April; nor was Vincent himself in London when it eventually did. In mid-May, he was transferred again, at first temporarily, but then permanently, to the Paris branch. On Monday 24 May, An Exhibition of High-Class Continental Pictures, containing Specimens of Gérôme, Meissonier, Jules Breton, Hébert, Millet, Corot, Troyon, Fortuny, Agrasot, Villegas, Sorby etc, opened at 25, Bedford Street, Strand. It was as if the whole point of Vincent's coming to London two years previously had been annulled.

3 *Ramsgate*

Vincent spent two months in Ramsgate as a teacher in the school of Mr Stokes (see below). He arrived on Easter Sunday, 16 April 1876; he left on Monday, 12 June.

Nine letters survive from this stay, each of them dated. An undated letter (LT68) has been put among this dated sequence, inferring that Vincent walked the seventy miles to London one Saturday in order to see Gladwell – and, the more embellished accounts add – Eugenie Loyer. Not only was the walk from Ramsgate to London impossible in one day, but LT68 must be placed among the letters from Isleworth. (i) Van Iterson, a former Goupil colleague in The Hague, could have easily visited Vincent at Isleworth on one of his business trips to London. (ii) Moreover, in LT75, dated 30 October 1876, he speaks of the drawings that van Iterson had brought with him, and continues:" Has van Iterson come back yet? I was so glad to see him again. He is bringing you *The Wide, Wide World*." This book was promised to Theo in LT68: clearly, to save postage, Vincent asked van Iterson to take it with him. (iii) The visit to London mentioned in LT68 took place on Saturday 23 September: it is recalled in LT75. All this suggests that LT68, a short, hurried note written in pencil, must date from about 19 or 20 September; its place in the *Letters* is therefore before LT75.

Vincent never left Ramsgate during his two months' sojourn there – at least he went no further than Pegwell Bay. When Mr Stokes decided to transfer his school to Isleworth it seems probable that Vincent couldn't afford the fare to London. Instead, he chose to walk, leaving Ramsgate on Monday 12 June and eventually, after two nights in London, visiting his sister Anna in Welwyn. He probably spent at least one night at Welwyn and from there went directly to Isleworth. The walk from Ramsgate to London took place once, and was one-way only.

The nine dated letters from Ramsgate contain some of Vincent's earliest – and finest – descriptive passages on landscape. Perhaps this burgeoning talent emerged so clearly in Ramsgate partly because he was starved of the paintings that had been so much a part of his life for the past three years: he needed a substitute outlet and the challenge of literary description provided it. On his first day in Ramsgate, he took a walk by the sea:

> The houses near the sea are mostly built of yellow brick in the style of those in the Nassaulaan in The Hague, but they are higher and have gardens full of cedars and other dark

Photograph of Vincent, January 1873

Vincent gives the London address of Goupil (LT 7, 5 May 1873)

Copy after De Nittis (LT 32, Paris, 24 July 1875)

van Gogh HACKFORD ROAD, BRIXTON   Pencil, heightened with white on prepared paper, 11.5 × 16.5 cm

Dit kerkje is een merkwaardig overblijfsel van eene oude Augustyner stichting (Austin friars) minstens reeds dateerende van het jaar 1354 zoomel reeds een 100 jaren vroeger Reeds sedert 1550 ingevolge van eene vrijwillige schenking van Eduard VI houdt de Nederduitsche gemeente hier hare Godsdienstige samenkomsten.

van Gogh AUSTIN FRIARS Pen, 10 × 17 cm

van Gogh RAMSGATE – VIEW FROM 6 ROYAL ROAD Pen and pencil, 5.5 × 5.5 cm

van Gogh RAMSGATE – VIEW FROM 6 ROYAL ROAD Pen and pencil, 6.5 × 10.5 cm
Enclosed with LT 67, 31 May 1876

Detail from Postcard of Ramsgate, c1905

View from 6 Royal Road, Ramsgate, 1974

van Gogh HOUSES AT ISLEWORTH 14 × 14.5 cm

Garden front of Holme Court, Isleworth. Photograph, c1935

[Handwritten paragraph from Vincent's sermon]

Paragraph from Vincent's sermon, delivered in Richmond on Sunday, 5 November 1876

PETERSHAM AND TURNHAM GREEN CHURCHES   Pen and pencil, 4 × 10 cm. Part of LT 82, 25 November 1876

[Handwritten postcard]

Postcard sent to Theo from The Hague, Tuesday, 2 May 1882 (LT 196)

evergreens. There is a harbour full of ships enclosed by stone jetties on which one can walk. (LT 61, 17 April 1876)

This exploratory walk gave him his first view of Pugin's house, *The Grange*, as well as St Augustine and its neighbour, Chartham Terrace. He was but two minutes away in Royal Road, yet remained unaware of Pugin's architectural presence. In a letter to his parents, he speaks of the houses being in simple Gothic style. A few days later he described a longer walk he took with the boys (LT 63, 28 April 1876):

> Now I am going to tell you about a walk we took yesterday. It was to an inlet of the sea, and the road there led through fields of young corn and along hedges of hawthorn, etc. Once there, we saw to our left a steep two-storey-high ridge of sand and stone. On top of it were old gnarled hawthorn bushes – their black and grey moss-covered stems and branches were all bent to one side by the wind; there were also a few elder bushes. The ground we walked on was all covered with big grey stones, chalk and shells. To the right lay the sea as calm as a pond, reflecting the light of the transparent grey sky where the sun was setting. The tide was out and the water very low.

This is clearly a walk to Pegwell Bay; parts of the letter make an appropriate accompaniment to Dyce's famous painting (Tate Gallery). But it was another artist whom Vincent used to sharpen the description of a storm (LT 67, 31 May 1876).

> The sea was yellowish, especially near the shore; on the horizon a strip of light, and above it immense dark grey clouds from which the rain poured down in slanting streaks. The wind blew the dust from the little white path on the rocks into the sea and bent the blooming hawthorn bushes and wallflowers that grow on the rocks. To the right were fields of young green corn, and in the distance the town looked like the towns Albrecht Dürer used to etch. A town with its turrets, mills, slate roofs and houses built in Gothic style, and below, the harbour between two jetties which project far into the sea.

And he continued in the same letter:

> From the window of my room that same night I looked on the roofs of the houses that can be seen from there and on the tops of the elm trees, dark against the night sky. Over these roofs one single star, but a beautiful, large, friendly one.

This is the only description of the view from his own room – it suggests that he had an attic or top floor room at the rear of Royal Road. The two drawings that he made were taken from the first floor front balcony of the school at 6 Royal Road, looking out to sea (p 10). No description of his room; no list of prints that he hung there; little mention of reading – a reference to Eliot's *Silas Marner* is the only break from the Bible reading to the boys: no wonder he wrote later from Isleworth (LT 82a, early September 1876):

> Love the town in which you dwell, as you do, too – don't I love Paris and London, though I am a child of the pine woods and of the beach at Ramsgate.

4 *William Port Stokes (1832?–1890)*. When Vincent arrived in Ramsgate, Mr Stokes was not there.

> During his absence his place was taken by his son (23 years old, I think), a teacher in London. I saw Mrs Stokes at dinner.

Mr Stokes himself arrived five days later:

> He is a man of medium height, with bald head and whiskers; the boys seem to like yet respect him. A few hours after his homecoming he was playing marbles with them.

And less favourably, Vincent noted in his last letter from Ramsgate (LT 67, 31 May 1876):

> On such (rainy) days Mr Stokes is sometimes in a bad temper, and when the boys make more noise than he likes, they occasionally have to go without their supper.

The Rate Books in Ramsgate Public library reveal that W S (sic) Stokes occupied 6 Royal Road by July 1872. We know from Vincent's letters that he left Ramsgate in June 1876 and moved his school to Isleworth.

This move to Isleworth was quite simply a return home for Stokes. Although born in Hammersmith, probably in 1832, he was brought up at Isleworth. He married Lydia Blyth at All Saints, Isleworth on 25 January 1855; a daughter, christened Lydia Ann, was born on 6 August 1861. There is no trace of a son in the parish church registers: if Vincent were right, this son would have been born about 1853, before Stokes' marriage. However, more interesting is Stokes' profession. Already in the 1851 census, where his age is given as 17, he is called a "painter (artist)"; in 1855, his profession is given as "artist", in 1861 as "drawing master." And this same W P Stokes exhibited *one* picture in London: at the 1855 exhibition of the British Institution he showed 'The Mendicant' (no 416, price ten guineas). He was then living at Hook, Hampshire – this was soon after his marriage. His movements between 1861 and his arrival in Ramsgate in 1872 are so far untraced. He may well have continued his profession of drawing master, in which case he was simply following his father. James Stokes was a drawing master at Wrotham House, Brentford End, London Road, Isleworth, his home from 1849 to his death in 1865 in his 76th year. Clearly he was a much more successful artist than his son, exhibiting between 1846 and 1863 two works at the Royal Academy, twenty-one at the British Institution and two at the Society of British Artists. These were predominantly landscapes from Scotland, Ireland, Wales and several English counties.

On the other hand, W P Stokes could have combined his mother's profession with that of his father's. Ann Stokes ran, at the same Wrotham House, a preparatory school for girls (1862), a ladies' school (1867) and a boarding school for young gentlemen (1874 and 1878). When he returned to Isleworth in 1876, W P Stokes took a house on the Twickenham Road, called Linkfield House (now destroyed). His profession is given as schoolmaster in a directory of 1877. Ten years later he is still at the same address, running a boys' boarding and day school. He died on 4 September 1890, aged 58 years, according to his tombstone in All Saints' Churchyard; a tombstone that he shared with his father (died 30 October 1865) and his mother (died 29 January 1883, aged 77 years).

Presumably by 1876 Stokes had given up his artistic pretensions; presumably, too, he didn't disclose their existence to Vincent. Yet it does seem curious that Vincent's two drawings of Ramsgate should have been made in the house of a former drawing master.

VINCENT AND ENGLISH PAINTING

"I am curious to see the English painters; we see so little of them because almost everything remains in England," Vincent wrote from The Hague on 17 March 1873 (LT 5). This was fair comment: English artists didn't exhibit much in Holland or Belgium and, with one exception, they were not handled by Goupil. Vincent had spent two months in London before he gave his first reactions to English art. In a letter of 20 July 1873 (LT 10), he provided quite a lengthy assessment:

> At first English art did not appeal to me; one must get used to it. But there are clever painters here, among others, Millais, who has painted 'The Huguenot', 'Ophelia', etc, of which I think you know the engravings; his things are beautiful. Then there is Boughton, whose 'Puritans Going to Church' is in our Galerie Photographique; I have seen wonderful things by him. Among the old painters, Constable was a landscape painter who lived about thirty years ago; he is splendid – his work reminds me of Diaz and Daubigny. Then there are Reynolds and Gainsborough, whose forte was very beautiful ladies' portraits, and Turner, whose engravings you must have seen. Some good French painters live here, including Tissot of whose work there are several photographs in our Galerie Photographique.

It's a short and fairly predictable list of Old Masters. But there are some odd features. This is the only reference Vincent ever makes to Turner – and then only to the *Liber Studorium*. Nor does he mention Gainsborough again, even though he would see more examples at Dulwich and the National Gallery. Reynolds, too, only gets another brief citation as one of several exhibitors in the Academy's Winter Exhibition of 1875. Vincent's reaction to Constable is again predictable for the period. The comparison with Diaz and Daubigny is one that was often made, although the more chauvinistic English critics always did so to the disadvantage of the French painters. For Vincent, the link was made freshly and without *parti pris*; he arrived in London already aware of Diaz and Daubigny, both of whom were handled by Goupil, and Constable's work reminded him of theirs.

One of the regrettable gaps in Vincent's surviving letters from England is the dearth of references to his visits to national and other permanent collections in and around London. Even when he visited Dulwich in August 1873 he doesn't mention a single painting. Only when he visited Hampton Court in June 1876 did he bother to give Theo some indication of the pictures he saw there:

> Among other things there are many portraits by Holbein which are very beautiful; two splendid Rembrandts (the portrait of his wife, and of a rabbi); beautiful Italian portraits by Bellini, Titian; a picture by Leonardo da Vinci; cartoons by Mantegna, a beautiful picture by S Ruysdael; a still-life of fruit by Cuyp, etc.

From the letters of 1873–76, there is not the slightest indication of his having visited the National Gallery or South Kensington. Much later, however, in August 1884, when Theo is planning to visit London, Vincent writes:

> Just notice the Hobbema in the National Gallery; you must not forget a few very beautiful Constables there, including 'Cornfield', nor that other one in South Kensington called 'Valley Farm'. (LT 374)

So the early mention of Constable is given more substance. This passage shows that he had looked hard in both the National Gallery and at South Kensington a decade earlier. It is also interesting for the pair of paintings that he singles out. Perhaps one ought to look a little more closely at some of Vincent's own landscapes of Nuenen and elsewhere for the occasional reminder of Constable. His only other reference to the English landscape painter was made after a walk by the Thames in August 1876 when he found the sky "such as Ruysdael or Constable would have painted."

The only exhibition of Old Masters that Vincent actually mentions during his first London stay is the Winter Exhibition of 1875 at Burlington House. After referring to Rembrandt, Ruysdael, Hals, Van Dyck, Rubens, Titian and Tintoretto in "this beautiful exhibition of old art", he concludes, "and some beautiful old English art – Reynolds, Romney, and a splendid 'Old Crome' landscape." (LT 22). Reynolds gets his second, Romney his only mention. Far more revealing is Vincent's reference to "a splendid 'Old Crome' landscape." In a letter to *The Athenaeum* of 9 January 1875, Charles W. Deschamps wrote: "In the present Exhibition of works by the Old Masters there is a picture, No 215, 'A Landscape, Evening', which is attributed to Old Crome, whereas the scene is a wooded slope of Montmartre, the painter Georges Michel, a French artist of the last century . . . I know of several fine examples of Georges Michel which are carelessly pronounced to be the works of the better-known John Crome." This question of attribution becomes doubly interesting for Vincent. In the letter that follows the one describing the Old Crome landscape, he writes enthusiastically of George Eliot's *Adam Bede:*

> The landscape in which the fallow sandy path runs over the hill to the village with its clay or whitewashed cottages and moss-covered roofs, and with an occasional blackthorn bush on either side of the brown heath and a gloomy sky with a narrow white streak at the horizon – it is like one by Michel. But there is an even purer and nobler sentiment in it than in Michel. (LT 23, 6 March 1875)

Clearly the "Old Crome" landscape that he saw at Burlington House could also have acted as an illustration to the passage in *Adam Bede*. The Academy's confusion of Crome and Michel becomes for Vincent a surprising unity of mood and encounter. In a later letter of December 1882 (LT 251), he talks of artists and of pictures that are simple, true and honest:

> How much good it does one to see a beautiful Rousseau on which he has drudged to keep it true and honest. How much good it does to think of people like Van Goyen, Old Crome and Michel.

How odd that Crome and Michel are placed together in this brief list! And all the more so as this is the only other occasion after February 1875 that Vincent mentions Crome. It seems certain that he was recalling the "splendid" landscape that he saw then. His retentive visual memory, as so often, is joined to his compelling need to group and categorize.

Constable, a 'wrong' Old Crome, and Turner's engravings: it's not the most complete list of English landscape artists. And what of the English watercolourists? One artist alone has to fill the gaps: Richard Parkes Bonington. Bonington's name first appears in a list of over fifty favourite artists that Vincent compiled in January 1874 – the only other English artists being Millais and Boughton. After that Bonington's name flits through Vincent's letters up to 1882. First, he hangs a print, 'Une Route', on the wall of his room in Paris in July 1875 (LT 30) – the only English print among a bevy of Dutch and French. Secondly, he sends Theo two lithographs after Bonington (LT 35, 2 September 1875). He doesn't tell us which. Thirdly (LT 36 4 September 1875), he assesses him: his test of quality is the mysterious *it*. "There is also a painting by Bonington which is almost *it*, but *not quite*." Again, he doesn't tell us which. Fourthly, in his last letter from Amsterdam in May 1878 (LT 122), he talks of the bad weather there, and thinks it will probably be the same in Paris. Theo had just moved to Paris from The Hague. Vincent continues: "You will soon perceive that it is much warmer there in summer than in Holland, and you will also see thundery skies like the ones Bonington painted." The final reference occurs in a letter from The Hague of July 1882 (LT 212). In response to Theo's description of Paris by night, Vincent writes: "there is a *je ne sais quoi* in your description, a fragrance, a memory, for instance, of a watercolour by Bonington – only it is still vague, as if in a haze."

These references to Bonington neatly illustrate the different ways in which Vincent "quarries" an artist he admires. He collects prints to hang in his room and to send to his brother; he provides an assessment – not quite *it*; he isolates a characteristic aspect of the artist's handling and uses it vividly to illustrate a physical event – here an effect of thundery sky, a reference that adds further interest to some of his own thundery skies in several Paris cityscapes of 1886–87; and finally, a literary description evokes a responsive pictorial analogy.

What of living British artists of the 1870's? What of the Royal Academy Summer Exhibition? Vincent visited that of 1873 and wrote of it in the context of an exhibition of Belgian painting which he had just seen (LT 11, 13 September 1873):

> It was a real pleasure to see those Belgian pictures; the English ones are with a few exceptions very bad and uninteresting. Some time ago I saw one which represented a kind of fish or dragon, six yards long. It was awful. And then a little man, who came to kill the above-mentioned dragon. I think the whole represented 'The Archangel Michael Killing Satan' . . . Another English picture is 'Satan Possessing the Herd of Swine at the Lake of Gadarena'. It represented about 50 black pigs and swine running helter-skelter down the mountain, and skipping over one another into the sea. But there was a very clever picture by Prinsep.

This light-hearted, mocking tone, is unusual for Vincent. The first painting he singled out for this dismissive treat-

Boughton   CHRISTMAS MORNING IN THE OLDEN TIME   *ILN Christmas Supplement, 1870*

Millais   THE NORTH-WEST PASSAGE
RA 1874 (320)   *The Tate Gallery, London*

Boughton   THE HEIR   RA 1873 (1062)

Millais   THE HUGUÉNOT   Mezzotint by
T O Barlow

Millais   CHILL OCTOBER   RA 1871 (14)   *Private Collection, England*

Poynter   FIGHT BETWEEN MORE OF MORE HALL AND THE DRAGON OF WANTLEY: COMPANION PICTURE TO PERSEUS AND ANDROMEDA
RA 1873 (541)

Walker   THE WAYFARERS   Etching

Tissot   VIEW OF SHIPPING FROM A ROOM   Drawn in Ramsgate,
1876.   *The Tate Gallery, London*

Tissot   THE BALL ON SHIPBOARD   RA 1874 (690)   *The Tate
Gallery, London*

Hobbema   THE AVENUE, MIDDELHARNIS   *The National Gallery, London*

Constable   THE CORNFIELD   *The National Gallery, London*

Constable   THE VALLEY FARM: WILLY LOTT'S HOUSE   *The Tate Gallery, London*

Feyen-Perrin LUNE DE MIEL *Goupil Galerie Photographique*

Brion LES ADIEUX *Musée Goupil et Cie*

Title Page of 5th Annual Exhibition,
Goupil Gallery, London 1879

ment was Poynter's 'Fight between More of More Hall and the Dragon of Wantley'. The subject is taken from Percy's *Reliques* and was one of four works commissioned from Poynter by the Earl of Wharncliffe for the decoration of his billiard-room at Wharncliffe Hall, near Sheffield. From his mis-reading of the action of this picture, it would seem that Vincent went round the exhibition without a catalogue. The other painting he describes is 'The Gadarene Swine' by Prinsep. And as Prinsep had exhibited two other pictures, it is not easy to know which was the "very clever picture" by him.

However, there was one painting in the Academy of 1873 that greatly attracted him, although he didn't speak of it until much later. He wrote to his painter friend Rappard from The Hague in November 1882 (R 19):

> I know Boughton's 'The Heir' as a painting; I saw it at the Royal Academy and later at Goupil's. At the time I admired it so much that I made a little sketch of it for an acquaintance in Holland, to give him an idea of it. I do not know the wood-engraving.

'The Heir' (No 1062) was Boughton's only painting in the Academy of 1873. Vincent's sketch of it for his Dutch friend must be among his earliest documented copies. And it was as a Goupil picture that Henry James saw it in New York in 1875, when he praised its landscape, but criticized the infelicity of the figures.

It was also Boughton who dominated Vincent's memory of the Academy exhibition of 1874. Again, however, he didn't mention this at the time. He was briefer but kinder than he had been the previous year:

> There are beautiful things in the Royal Academy this year. Tissot has three pictures there." (LT 17, 16 June 1874)

Among the Tissots was the Tate Gallery's 'The Ball on Shipboard'. Vincent first described the Boughton in a letter from Isleworth of 26 August 1876 (LT 74):

> Did I ever tell you about that picture by Boughton, 'The Pilgrim's Progress?' It is toward evening. A sandy path leads over the hills to a mountain, on the top of which is the Holy City, lit by the red sun setting behind the grey evening clouds. On the road is a pilgrim who wants to go to the city; he is already tired and asks a woman in black, who is standing by the road and whose name is "Sorrowful yet always rejoicing": Does the road go uphill all the way?
> "Yes, to the very end."
> And will the journey take all day long?
> "Yes, from morn till night, my friend."
> The landscape through which the road winds is so beautiful –brown heath, and occasional birches and pine trees and patches of yellow sand, and the mountain far in the distance, against the sun. Truly, it is not a picture, but an inspiration.

The misquotation from Christina Rossetti has often been noted; the misinterpretation of Boughton hasn't. Vincent is referring to Boughton's only painting in the Academy of 1874: No 982 'God speed! Pilgrims setting out for Canterbury: time of Chaucer'. It has so far proved impossible to locate this picture, or to find a photograph or an engraving of it. But descriptions in several contemporary reviews clearly establish that Vincent was confusing a spring evocation of Chaucer's pilgrims leaving a now distant London with an image of Bunyan's pilgrim striving towards the Holy City on an autumnal evening. Yet so fixed was his own interpretation of the painting, so strong his feeling for its inspirational quality, that he used it as the peroration of his sermon in November 1876. In his sermon, he elaborates on the description already given in his letter to Theo. And on his last recorded visit to London from Isleworth, he called on his former Goupil boss Mr Obach and saw "the picture or rather sketch, by Boughton, 'The Pilgrim's Progress'."

Vincent's affair with George Henry Boughton (1834–1905), a now virtually forgotten Victorian artist, continued until the early 1880's. It began with his deep admiration for Boughton as the illustrator of Longfellow and of the Puritans in New England; it ended with his reading of articles on Holland by Boughton, with illustrations by the latter and E A Abbey, that appeared in *Harper's Magazine* in 1883. "I think 'In the Potato Field' the most beautiful of all, and the 'Bell Ringers' by Abbey. Text somewhat dry, somewhat cluttered with stories about hotels and antique dealers—I enjoy reading it," Vincent wrote to Rappard in July 1883. He admired the paintings largely for their literary basis, their historical revivalism, their pastoral gentility. But Boughton was also handled by Goupil and his paintings reproduced in their Galerie Photographique. Vincent the young art dealer clearly held him in great esteem. He later recalled from Drenthe (LT 332, 20 October 1883):

> In London how often I stood drawing on the Thames Embankment, on my way home from Southampton Street in the evening, and it came to nothing. If there had been somebody then to tell me what perspective was, how much misery I should have been spared, how much further I should be now! Well, let bygones be bygones. It has not been so. I spoke one or twice to Thijs Maris. I dared not speak to Boughton because his presence overawed me.

He once saw another English artist in London. He recalled this in a letter to Theo from Amsterdam (LT 102, 15 July 1877):

> Once I met the painter Millais on the street in London, just after I had been lucky enough to see several of his pictures. And that noble figure reminded me of John Halifax. Millais once painted 'The Lost Mite', a young woman who early in the morning, at dawn, is looking for the mite she has lost (there is also an engraving of 'The Lost Mite'), and not the least beautiful of his pictures is an autumn landscape, 'Chill October'.

Elsewhere, he mentions other works by Millais. For example, he sends Theo a photograph of 'The Huguenot' in February 1877 to hang in his little room. In The Hague in December 1882 (LT 249), he recalls 'The North-West Passage', which he had seen at The Royal Academy of 1874, and paraphrases what was written beneath the picture, "It might be done, and if so, we should do it." But the one painting by Millais that captured his imagination was 'Chill October'. He mentions it on four different occasions between July 1877 and August 1884, always in terms of approbation. "For my part," he tells Theo in August 1884 (LT 374), "I have always remembered some English pictures such as 'Chill October' by Millais." He tells Rappard in May 1882 (R 8) that "Mauve was quite thrilled when he saw Millais's landscape, 'Chill October'." Mauve must have seen it at the Paris International Exhibition of 1878. But where had Vincent himself seen it?

Painted in 1870 – Millais's first pure landscape – 'Chill October' was exhibited at the Royal Academy of 1871 and bought by Samuel Mendel of Manchester. The only occasion when Vincent could have seen it during his stay in London was at the Mendel sale at Christie's on 24 April 1875. Its attraction for him was clearly its sentiment: "It does what all good landscape should do – embodies a sentiment and expresses a feeling," wrote *The Times* art critic in 1871. Vincent had written in a letter from London in October 1873 (LT 11a): "It is worth noting that the old painters hardly ever painted autumn, and that the modern ones have a predilection for it." Season, simplicity of statement, and sentiment all attracted Vincent – as they must have attracted Mauve. And there seems to be a distant echo of 'Chill October' in two of Vincent's early drawings done at Etten in the summer of 1881 (F 845–46).

Boughton and Millais dominated Vincent's view of English painting. During his stay in London, the other artists he admired were exiles like himself – Tissot and Matthew Maris. In his post-English letters, he tells us a little more about the work of two other exiles – Whistler and Legros. He talks primarily of their etchings, of their portraits of Carlyle and of having seen their work in London exhibitions. His opinions on Whistler and Legros, as well as Tissot and Maris, don't add materially to his view of English painting.

However, there are two artists whose work he evidently saw and admired in London. When recalling Hobbema,

Constable and Millais's 'Chill October', he also remembered "the drawings by Fred Walker and Pinwell." (LT 374, August 1884). And he wrote further of Pinwell (LT 262, January 1882):

> He was such a poet that he saw the sublime in the most ordinary, commonplace things. His work is rare – I saw very little of it, but that little was so beautiful that now, at least ten years later, I see it as clearly as I did the first time.

Neither Pinwell nor Walker exhibited at the Royal Academy in 1873 or 1874. Vincent could have seen some of their work at the exhibitions of the watercolour societies. He refers to their watercolours elsewhere (LT 297, July 1883), noting that "the outlines are very strongly expressed." This was a much-noticed feature of the watercolour technique of Walker and his followers, often attributed to their experience as designers for wood-engraving. But it is an etching by Walker that Vincent specifically describes in a letter to Rappard of 28 May 1882 (R 8):

> Do you know 'The Wayfarers' by Fred Walker? It is a large etching of a blind old man led by a boy along a frozen gravel road, with a ditch along which there is copse-wood covered with glazed frost, on a winter evening. It certainly is one of the most sublime creations in this style, with a very peculiar modern sentiment, perhaps less powerful than Dürer in his 'Knight, Death and the Devil', but perhaps even more intimate, and certainly as original and sincere.

His last reference to Walker and Pinwell comes appropriately in a letter from Nuenen of May 1885 (LT 406), when he himself was fully occupied with his drawings and paintings of peasants:

> I just read an article in the *Graphic* on an exhibition of twenty-five drawings by Fred Walker. Walker died some ten years ago, you know. Pinwell too – while I'm on this subject, I'm thinking of their work too, and how very clever they were. How they did in England exactly what Maris, Israëls, Mauve, have done in Holland, namely restored nature over convention; sentiment and impression over academic platitudes and dullness. How they were the first tonists. But I remember peasants in the field by Pinwell, 'The Harbour of Refuge' by Walker, of which one might also say, *peints avec de la terre*.

A fitting valediction: not merely for its quotation from Sensier's book on Millet, whom Walker had also admired, but for its tie-up of the English artists' achievements with those of The Hague School. But then it was 1885, and Vincent was shedding his English interests, moving towards Delacroix, Rubens, the Japanese Print and Impressionism.

Millais and Boughton, Walker and Pinwell, Poynter and Prinsep, with the four exiles, Maris, Tissot, Legros and Whistler: it's not the most inclusive view of the state of painting in England in the 1870's. No mention of Rossetti or Burne-Jones, of Leighton or Albert Moore – and none, incidentally, of Ruskin and Pater. Yet there seems to be a hint of awareness of the Pre-Raphaelites. Soon after his arrival in London, Vincent read Keats' poems: "He is the favourite of all the painters here, and so I started reading him." (LT 10a, 7 August 1873). But then nothing more on Keats. In 1877, a brief reference to the unnamed artist who painted 'The Light of the World'. Then nothing until November 1889 in St Rémy when he is discussing the problems of painting Biblical subjects (LT 614):

> And the Pre-Raphaelites too went a long way in this category of ideas. When Millais (sic) painted his 'Light of the World', it was a more serious matter. Really there is no comparison. Without counting Holman Hunt and others – Pinwell and Rossetti.

And that's all he wrote on the Pre-Raphaelites. But he may have been thinking of them and some of their imitators when he wrote in October 1876 from Isleworth (LT 78) that "many painters and graphic artists here work in the style of Holbein."

Another group of artists – a very loosely knit group – escaped his attention altogether. There is no mention of the 'social realist' pictures that were shown at the Academy from 1873 to 1875. These included Frank Holl's 'Leaving Home' (RA 1873) and 'Deserted' (1874), Luke Fildes's 'Applicants for Admission to a Casual Ward' (1874) and Herkomer's 'The Last Muster' (1875). The explanation must surely be that Vincent wasn't then ready for 'social realist' subject matter and technique. He was still a Goupil man, much conditioned by his four years in The Hague. He liked his art to be historical-revivalist (Leys, early Tissot), "melancholic-modern" in landscape (Millais), gently illustrative (Boughton) and slightly tougher, but still "poetic" in its treatment of modern subjects (Walker and Pinwell). The stronger realism of Holl, Fildes and Herkomer left him unmoved. The "conversion" was wrought in the experiences of his own life, in his reading, and, ultimately, in his acquisition of past numbers of the *Graphic* and the *Illustrated London News*. He viewed English illustrators in quite a different way from English painters.

VINCENT AND THE VICTORIAN NOVEL: DICKENS AND ELIOT

Vincent's reading of the Victorian novelists wasn't wide-ranging; and those few he did read were often discovered fortuitously. For example, he read Bulwer-Lytton's *Kenelm Chillingly* in Paris in March 1876 because it was given to him by an aunt.

> It is really fine – the adventures of a rich Englishman's son who could find no rest or peace in his own sphere and tried to find it among the lower classes. In the end he returned to his own class, but did not regret his experiences (LT 56).

Yet he seems not to have followed this up with other novels of Bulwer-Lytton, although he kept Laugée's wood-engraved portrait from the *Graphic*.

By chance, he came across Charlotte Brontë's *Shirley* at his uncle Vincent's house in June 1881. He wrote to Theo:

> I do not know if you ever read English books; if you do, I can strongly recommend that you read *Shirley* by Currer Bell, author of another book called *Jane Eyre*. It is as beautiful as pictures by Millais, or Boughton or Herkomer. I found it at Prinsenhage and finished it in three days, though it is quite a voluminous book. (LT 148)

He *may* have followed this up by reading *Jane Eyre*.

It seems certain that he never read Thackeray (true, there is an oblique mention through the eyes of Gavarni) or Mrs Gaskell. He did read Mrs Craik's *John Halifax, Gentleman* and Susan Warner's *The Wide Wide World* – fairly early on in his career, one must point out. Both Trollope and Hardy escaped his net, yet both were serialised in the *Graphic* – in Trollope's case illustrated by Frank Holl, one of Vincent's favourite English artists. Henry James escaped him too; it's odd to think of each of them in Paris in 1876, the one exercising his secondary role of art critic, the other waiting to escape from art dealing.

In fact, his view of Victorian literature is really confined to three authors: George Eliot, Dickens and Carlyle. For various reasons, Carlyle will be left out of the discussion. Towards Eliot and Dickens he was extremely serious, keen to find their books, anxious to pass them on to his parents and friends, ever ready to pass judgements, make comparisons, identify with their characters and situations, and generally enter into their imaginative experience. Yet for all that, he keeps them separate, only four times mentioning them in the same letter, only twice in the same sentence. This suggests that Vincent *kept* their worlds apart, or *saw* them as worlds apart; or simply that he read them at different periods and thus avoided any possible overlap. Whatever the answer, there is every justification for treating them separately, beginning with Eliot.

Vincent wrote to Theo from Amsterdam on 3 March 1878:

Have you read any good books lately? Be sure you read the works of George Eliot, you will not regret it: *Adam Bede, Silas Marner, Felix Holt, Romola* (Savonarola's life), *Scenes from* (sic) *Clerical Life.* When I again have time for reading, I shall certainly reread them. (LT 120)

The first thing to say is that Vincent apparently didn't read the whole of Eliot: *The Mill on the Floss* and *Daniel Deronda*, for example, are never mentioned by him. Rather, he concentrated on four works: *Adam Bede, Scenes of Clerical Life, Silas Marner* and *Felix Holt.* The sequence of discovery can be followed. He first read *Adam Bede* in London in 1875. Between January and March 1876 in Paris he read *Felix Holt, Scenes of Clerical Life* and almost certainly *Silas Marner*. If he actually read *Romola*, he never tells us when. It could have been in Amsterdam in 1877–78, when he could have used the novel as substitute history. There's evidence of some re-reading between 1878 and 1883 (eg in Etten in December 1881). But the next clear indication is the first reading of *Middlemarch* in February 1883. And apart from the re-reading of *Felix Holt* at Nuenen in 1884, that's it.

His attitudes towards the novels were often conditioned by the moment that he chose to read them. For instance, a description of landscape in *Adam Bede* echoes his current admiration for the French painter Georges Michel. The concentrated reading that he did in Paris in the early months of 1876 might possibly have been sparked off by his English friend, Harry Gladwell. But the passages he chose to quote have strong autobiographical overtones. Thus, he wrote to Theo on 19 February 1876:

> I have just read a very fine book by Eliot, *Scenes of Clerical Life;* three tales especially the last one, *Janet's Repentance,* struck me very much. It is the story of a clergyman who lived chiefly among the inhabitants of the squalid streets of a town; his study looked out on gardens with cabbage stalks, etc, and on the red roofs and smoking chimneys of poor tenements. For his dinner he usually had nothing but underdone mutton and watery potatoes. He died at the age of thirty-four. During his long illness he was nursed by a woman who had been a drunkard, but by his teaching, and leaning as it were on him, had conquered her weakness and found rest for her soul. At his burial they read the chapter which says, "I am the resurrection, and the life: he that believeth in me, though he were dead, yet shall he live."

In some measure, Vincent appears to self-identify with the evangelist Tryan. Not surprisingly; at this period, he was zealously reading the Bible, frequently attending an English church in Paris, and seriously thinking of becoming an evangelist or missionary himself. Indeed, a few months later in London, he applied for such a post among the labouring poor. He knew well the poor of Paris: "there is something in Paris more beautiful than the autumn and the churches and that is the poor." (LT 75). His room in Montmartre might well have looked out on "gardens with cabbage stalks, etc . . . and smoking chimneys of poor tenements." Later, his own attempt to 'save' the prostitute, Sien, with whom he lived in The Hague in 1882–83, is something of a transcription of the theme of *Janet's Repentance.* In The Hague also he will find a parallel to the burial scene in an illustration by Frank Holl.

He finds a further echo of his mid-seventies evangelism in *Silas Marner*:

> There is such a longing for religion among the people in the large cities . . . In one of her novels Eliot describes the life of factory workers who have formed a small community and hold their services in a chapel in Lantern Yard; she calls it the "kingdom of God on earth" – no more and no less.

In the mid-seventies, then, Eliot strengthens his social conscience and spurs his evangelical spirit. Later, however, with his own gathering scepticism and the broadening scope of his reading, he notes her position as a modern thinker, one of those "at the head of modern civilization." (LT 160). In one of his rare later references, he can compare her with Tolstoy:

> I am reading an article in the *Revue des deux Mondes* on Tolstoy. It appears that Tolstoy is enormously interested in the religion of his race, like George Eliot in England. (LT 542 August 1888)

And he can make one other broad comparison. He first read *Middlemarch* in February 1883, conceivably because he had read reviews of the novel in issues of the *Graphic* of 1871–72, which he had just acquired. Regrettably, he says nothing about the novel itself:

> I am reading Eliot's *Middlemarch.* Eliot analyses like Balzac or Zola – but English situations, with an English sentiment. (LT 267, c15 February 1883)

Appropriately, Vincent's longest passage on Eliot enables him to proclaim his admiration for *Felix Holt.* He is writing to Rappard from Nuenen in March 1884:

> The other day I re-read *Felix Holt, the Radical* by Eliot. This book has been very well translated into Dutch . . . There are certain conceptions of life in it that I think are excellent – deep things, said in a guilelessly humorous way; the book is written with great vigour, and various scenes are described in the same way Frank Holl or someone like him would draw them. The conception and the outlook are similar. There aren't many writers who are as thoroughly sincere and good as Eliot. This book *The Radical* is not so well known in Holland as her *Adam Bede,* for instance, and her *Scenes of Clerical Life* are not so well known either.

He defines elsewhere the character of Felix Holt himself as reflected in that of a Dutch artist acquaintance:

> There is something broad and rough in him which appeals to me very much – something of the roughness of torchon. A man who apparently doesn't seek culture in outward things, but who is inwardly much, very much further than most. (LT 280, 21 April 1883)

Couldn't this also stand as a self-portrait? And the identification seems complete when he compares Sien and her family to the following passage in *Felix Holt*:

> The people I live among have the same follies and vices as the rich, only they, *have their own forms* of folly and vice – and they have not what are called the *refinements* of the rich to make their faults more bearable. It does not much matter to me – I am not fond of those refinements, but some people are, and find it difficult to feel at home with such persons as have them not. (Quoted in LT 272, c4 March 1883)

Six years later, in St. Rémy, it is hardly surprising that Vincent should use *Felix Holt* to convince his sister Wil of the effect of simplicity he had tried to achieve in the painting of his bedroom.

It is clear that Vincent had read *some* of Dickens before he came to England in May 1873. Speaking of *A Christmas Carol* and *The Haunted Man,* he wrote:

> I have re-read these two "children's tales" nearly every year ever since I was a boy, and they are new to me again every time. (R 30, March 1883)

And writing to his parents in November 1876 (LT 81), he told them of an intended visit to Whitechapel, "that very poor part which you have read about in Dickens."

Yet oddly enough, this last reference is the only one he makes to Dickens throughout his stay in England. And we cannot be sure of the extent of his reading in Dickens by the time he left London in December 1876. In Holland he could recall Bookseller's Row, "where one sees everything – from etchings by Rembrandt to the Household Edition of Dickens and the Chandos Classics." (LT 112, 30 October 1877). And he could misquote from *Pickwick:* "A strange old plant is the ivy green." (LT 84, 21 January 1877) – the only mention he makes of this novel. But his reading continued in Amsterdam:

> Uncle Cor has given me a *Child's History of England* by Dickens – I don't know if I already told you. The book is pure gold – one of the things I read in it was a description of the Battle of Hastings. I think if one reads carefully a few books by men like Motley and Dickens, and like Gruson's *Croisades,* one cannot help acquiring a good, simple eye for history in general. (LT 114, 25 November 1877).

In the Borinage he picks up a French edition of *Hard Times*:

> Did you ever read Dickens's *Les Temps difficiles*? I give you the title in French because there is a very good French translation at 1.25 francs published by Hachette: *Bibliothèque des meilleurs Romans étrangers*. It is excellent; in it the character of Stephen Blackpool, a working man, is most striking and sympathetic. (LT 131)

This was in August 1879. Later that month, he visited his parents in Etten. His mother reported: "He reads Dickens all day and speaks only when he is spoken to." Back in the Borinage, 1880 was the year of Sidney Carton: he mentions him in a letter of July (LT 133), and in another of 24 September (LT 136) he wrote:

> Meryon (the famous French etcher) is said to have had such a capacity for love that, like Dickens's Sidney Carton, he loved even the stones of certain places.

Yet this period of concentrated reading in 1879–80 was only a preparation for the future. The spasmodic references in the letters needed to be brought together into a meaningful entity. In The Hague he achieved this. From January 1882 to July 1883, he bombarded Theo and Rappard with comment after comment. He will still mention the reading of a novel – for instance, *Edwin Drood*, which he read in hospital in June 1882. He will still produce a long quotation: in May 1883 (R 35) he uses part of the preface to *Little Dorrit* as a forceful expression of "what goes on in the mind of a figure painter while he is working on a composition." He will still refer to characters from the novels: eg Doyce in *Little Dorrit*, "as a type of those whose principle is How to do it" (LT 251 December 1882). He will still find the occasional Dickensian phrase: "the circumlocution office" predictably turns up (LT 263, 3 February 1883). And he will still talk of Dickens the substitute historian, but now *The Tale of Two Cities* is a quarry for "splendid subjects for drawings out of that revolutionary period – not bearing on history proper, but rather incidents of everyday life and the appearance of things as they used to be." (R 36, c25 May 1883)

Beyond all this, however, three major things happened in The Hague: he read Forster's *Life*, he acquired a virtually complete set of the Household Edition, and he found past copies of the *Graphic*.

He read Forster's *Life* in November 1882 (R 17 and LT 241). This supplied him with background information, allowed him to quote Dickens on the painter's use of the model, and enabled him to see the point of the preface in the later editions of *Martin Chuzzlewit*.

More important than Forster, however, was the acquisition of the novels themselves. Vincent wrote to Rappard in March 1883 (R 30):

> By the way, I have a nearly complete French edition of Dickens, translated under the supervision of Dickens himself. I think you told me once that you could not enjoy all the English books by Dickens because of the sometimes complicated English, as for instance the miners' (sic) dialect in *Hard Times*. If you should ever want to read something of this French edition, it is at your disposal, and I am even willing to exchange the whole collection of Dickens's works in French for something else, if you should care to. I am thinking of gradually getting the English Household Edition.

The Household Edition appeared between 1871 and 1879. Vincent was already aware of its existence when he was in London. Now, in The Hague, its lavish number of illustrations dominated his view of the novels. It's not Cruikshank's illustrations to *Oliver Twist* that he praises, but those of J Mahoney (p 25). Above all, he praises Fred Barnard, the major contributor to the Household Edition. A letter to Rappard highlights his attitude:

> I bought a new sixpenny edition of Dickens's *Christmas Carol* and *The Haunted Man* (London, Chapman & Hall) this week, in which there are some seven illustrations, eg among other things, a *Secondhand Shop* by Barnard (p 25) ... Barnard understood Dickens well. The other day I saw

photographs again of some black-and white drawings by Barnard, a series of characters from Dickens's books; I saw *Mrs Gamp*, *Little Dorrit*, *Sikes*, *Sidney Carton* and some others. They are highly accentuated figures – most important, treated as cartoons . . . There is character too in the illustrations by John Leech and Cruikshank – but the Barnards are more intensively worked out. Nevertheless, Leech is strong on street urchins.

Vincent's acquisition of the *Graphics* gave him several points of reference. First, it provided him with Fildes's illustration of 'The Empty Chair' (p 24), enthusiastically reported to Theo in July 1882 (LT 220). This acquisition came shortly after he had been reading *Edwin Drood*: June and July 1882 were Fildes months. The connexions between Dickens, Fildes' *Edwin Drood* and 'The Empty Chair' were pointed out by Vincent in a letter of December 1882 (LT 252):

> I see Millais running to Charles Dickens with the first issue of the *Graphic*. Dickens was then in the evening of his life, he had a paralysed foot and walked with a kind of crutch. Millais says that while showing him Luke Fildes's drawing 'Homeless and Hungry' (sic), of poor people and tramps in front of a free overnight shelter, Millais said to Dickens, "Give him your *Edwin Drood* to illustrate," and Dickens said, "Very well." *Edwin Drood* was Dickens's last work, and Luke Fildes, brought into contact with Dickens through those small illustrations, entered his room on the day of his death, and saw his empty chair; and so it happened that one of the old numbers of the *Graphic* contained that touching drawing, *The Empty Chair*.

(Vincent's source for this information was partly in the text that accompanied Fildes's 'Houseless and Hungry' in the *Graphic Portfolio* of 1877.) And in the same letter he concluded:

> The sublime beginning of the *Graphic* was something like what Dickens was an author, what the Household Edition of his work.

Vincent himself carried the Dickens-Graphic, novelist-illustrator links even further. Appropriately, the references occur in two letters to Rappard, who had become, as it were, his fellow-student of English illustrators and of Dickens – at least in French translation. In March 1883 (R 30), he wrote:

> There is no writer, in my opinion, who is *so* much a painter and a black-and-white artist as Dickens. His figures are resurrections.

And earlier, in mid-September 1882 (R 13):

> For me the English black-and-white artists are to art what Dickens is to literature. They have exactly the same sentiment, noble and healthy, and one always returns to them . . . I am organizing my whole life so as to do the things of everyday life that Dickens describes and the artists I've mentioned draw.

Apart from an incidental reference in March 1884 (R 43), Vincent doesn't mention Dickens again until 1889. His re-reading of the *Christmas Books* and his inclusion of the volume in his portrait of 'L'Arlésienne' have already been noted. (There are, incidentally, several thorny problems connected with the *four* surviving portraits of 'L'Arlésienne', which do involve the *Christmas Books*, but these cannot be discussed here.)

During his stay in The Hague, Vincent re-lived George Eliot and *Janet's Repentance*, he re-lived Dickens's London and his own experiences of Whitechapel. The boundaries between literature and life, between painting and novel, were removed: the spirit of Felix Holt enters the drawing of a soup-kitchen, that of Dickens invades a watercolour of a third class waiting-room. Eliot and Dickens had sustained Vincent at different periods: Eliot in the mid-seventies in London and Paris, Dickens in the Borinage in the late seventies. But in The Hague they come together: never was their sustenance more important to him than then.

MISS OR MRS.?

BY WILKIE COLLINS

"Whipping up the skirt of her dress on her knee, she bent forward over it, and set herself industriously to the repair of the torn trimming."—*Second Scene*

Fildes   MISS OR MRS?   *Graphic Christmas Number 1871*

Fildes   THE EMPTY CHAIR, GAD'S HILL – NINTH OF JUNE 1870   *Graphic, Christmas Number 1870*

Ik zie Millais met het eerste Nº van de Graphic naar Chs Dickens beloopen Dickens was toen aan den avond van zyn leven had toen een verlamming aan den voet liep met een soort kruk millais zegt terwyle hy hem de teekening gaf aan Luke Fildes laat zen "HOMELESS & Hungry – arme lui & vagabonden voor een nachtverblyf – millais zegt tot Dickens geef hem uw Edwin Drood te illustreeren & Dickens zegt "best".

Edwin Drood was 't laatste werk van Dickens en Luke Fildes door die kleine illustratien in contact met D. gekomen. Komt in zyn kamer den dag van zyn dood – ziet zyn leegen stoel staan en zoo komt het dat een der oude Nº van Graphic bevat die treffende teekening.

The empty chair.

Empty chairs — er zyn er velen & zullen er nog meer komen en vroeger of later zullen in plaats van Herkomer Luke Fildes Frank Holl & William Small ze slechts blyven Empty chairs.

En toch zullen steeds de uitgevers & handelaars niet luisterende naar eene profetie als die van H.H. in dergelyke waarden als in hyzaund

van Gogh   Part of LT 252, c11 December 1882

Fildes   IN THE COURT   *Edwin Drood, 1870*

Fildes   SLEEPING IT OFF   *Edwin Drood 1870*

"WHAT DO YOU CALL THIS!" SAID JOE, "BED CURTAINS!"—*A Christmas Carol*, Stave iv.

Barnard   ILLUSTRATION TO "A CHRISTMAS CAROL"   *Household Edition, 1877*

HE SAT DOWN ON THE STONE BENCH OPPOSITE THE DOOR—Chap. lvi.

Mahoney   ILLUSTRATION TO "OLIVER TWIST"   *Household Edition 1871*

Part of LT 267, c15 February 1883, in which Vincent refers to his reading of George Eliot's Middlemarch.

"The little sketch enclosed is scrawled after a larger study which has a more melancholy expression. There is a poem by Thomas Hood, I think, telling of a rich lady who cannot sleep at night because when she went out to buy a dress during the day, she saw the poor seamstress – pale, consumptive, emaciated – sitting at work in a close room. And now she is conscience-stricken about her wealth, and starts up anxiously in the night. In short, it is the figure of a slender, pale woman, restless in the dark night." (LT 185, early April 1882)

The Great Lady

van Gogh THE GREAT LADY Pencil, pen and wash, 19.6 × 10.8 cm. Enclosed in LT 185, early April 1882

VINCENT AND ENGLISH ILLUSTRATION

I have read with great interest the account of your scheme for encouraging a feeling for art in National schools . . . I think for children between nine and 12 or 13 – the great mass of those in elementary schools – fairly good engravings, such as those in the *Graphic, Illustrated News*, etc, (not the coloured pictures) to be as conducive to the end desired as more finished pictures and photographs.
(Thomas Hardy. From a letter of 11 April 1883)

The most valuable art teaching I had at Fettes was acquired from a study of the early numbers of the *Graphic* newspaper, bound volumes of which were in my house library. There I used to copy from the works of Boyd Houghton, E J Gregory, W Small and others.
(A S Hartrick *A Painter's Pilgrimage* 1939)

Friday, 12 December 1873 . . . home by 6.30 to dinner, bringing the Christmas numbers of the *Graphic* and the *Illustrated News*, that my darling might please herself with the pictures.
(Derek Hudson Munby *Man of Two Worlds*, 1972)

The Royal Academy of England, in its annual publication, is now nothing more than a large coloured *Illustrated Times* folded in saloons, – the splendidest May number of the *Graphic*, shall we call it? That is to say, it is a certain quantity of pleasant, but imperfect, "illustration" of passing events, mixed with as much gossip of the past, and tattle of the future, as may be probably agreeable to a populace supremely ignorant of the one, and reckless of the other.
(John Ruskin *Academy Notes*, 1875)

Ces qualités d'exacte notation et d'indiscutable véracité, communes à la plupart des dessinateurs de talent d'outre-Manche, ont rendu le *Graphic*, le *London News* (sic) *Illustrated*, des journaux sans rivaux dans la presse illustrée des deux mondes.
(J-K Huysmans *L'Art Moderne*: review of Salon of 1881)

I have another decoration for my studio – I bought very cheaply some beautiful wood-engravings from the *Graphic*, in part prints not from the cliché but from the blocks themselves. Just what I have been wanting for years, drawings by Herkomer, Frank Holl, Walker, and others.
(Vincent Letter to Theo, 7 January 1882)

For me the English black-and-white artists are to art what Dickens is to literature. They have exactly the same sentiment, noble and healthy, and one always returns to them.
(Vincent Letter to Rappard, mid-September 1882)

It is very curious to hear some painters talk about what they call "illustrators," about Gavarni, for instance, or Herkomer. *Not* knowing anything about the matter is what makes up part of their so-called *general information*. Much good may it do them.
(Vincent Letter to Theo, early April 1882)

I didn't tell you that I have almost the whole *Graphic* complete now, from the very beginning in 1870. Of course, not everything, there is too much chaff – but the best things from it. When one sees, for instance, Herkomer's work, arranged together instead of scattered among many insignificant things, it is, in the first place, easier and more pleasant to look at, but in addition, one learns to distinguish the characteristics of the various masters, and the great difference between the draughtsmen.
(Vincent Letter to Theo, c21 March 1883)

Who knows Buckman, who knows the two Greens, who knows Régamey's drawings? Only a very few. Seen together, one wonders at that firmness of drawing, that personal character, that serious conception and that penetration and artistic elevation of the most ordinary figures and subjects found in the street, in the market place, in a hospital or an almshouse.
(Vincent Letter to Theo, c2 July 1883)

The brothers Theo and Vincent van Gogh made four important collections. The first was of Vincent's own work (including his letters), a truly joint enterprise. The second was of work by other artists, mostly friends (Gauguin, Barnard, Seurat), but including Monticelli and Daumier and other French, Dutch and Belgian painters: its origin was a mixture of acquisition by Theo, artist's gift, and exchange with Vincent. The third was of Japanese Prints, mostly collected in Paris between 1886 and 1888, and where Theo followed Vincent's unbounded enthusiasm. The fourth collection was a mixture of prints, photographs, books and periodicals. Prominent among these are some 1500 wood-engravings, mainly culled from the pages of French and English illustrated periodicals of the 1870's and the early 1880's. Theo greatly helped in the building up of the French section: being in Paris, he could often send them to Vincent in Holland. But he took no part in the making of the collection of English wood-engravings – except financially. This was made solely by Vincent, mostly during his stay in The Hague between January 1882 and September 1883. The collection is dominated by pages from the *Graphic* and the *Illustrated London News*. Why Vincent chose to make it then, what he thought of the illustrations, and to what extent they influenced his own work, are questions worth exploring.

Vincent clearly knew of the existence of the *Graphic* and the *Illustrated London News* during his stay in London. Their offices were nearby Goupils' and he must often have window-gazed. A few months after leaving London in 1876, he wrote to Theo from Amsterdam:

> Maybe you know the wood-engravings by Swain: he is a clever man, his studio is in such a pleasant part of London, not far from that part of the Strand where the offices of the illustrated papers (*The London News, Graphic,* etc) are. (LT 112, 30 October 1877)

He makes stronger claims in a letter to Rappard written from The Hague in February 1883:

> More than ten years ago, when I was in London, I used to go every week to the show windows of the printing offices of the *Graphic* and the *London News* to see the new issues. The impressions I got on the spot were so strong that, notwithstanding all that has happened to me since, the drawings are clear in my mind. Sometimes it seems to me that there is no stretch of time between those days and now – at least my enthusiasm for those things is rather stronger than it was even then. (R 20)

He had just acquired 21 volumes of the *Graphic*. He wrote to Rappard:

> While I was looking through them, all my memories of London ten years ago came back to me – when I saw them for the first time; they moved me so deeply that I have been thinking about them ever since, for instance Holl's 'The Foundling' and Herkomer's 'Old Women'. (R 23, late January 1883)

And yet again to Rappard, he wrote:

> . . . as I lived in England for fully three years, I learned much about them (the black-and-white artists) and their work by seeing a lot of what they did. Without having been in England for a long time it is hardly possible to appreciate them to the full. (R 13, mid-September 1882)

And when he had just acquired his very first copies of the *Graphic*, in January 1882, he told Theo:

> Just what I've been wanting for years, drawings by Herkomer, Frank Holl, Walker, and others. (LT 169, 7 January 1882)

It all appears cut and dried: a clear case of deep admiration and strongly retained impressions of the drawings with a long-cherished desire to own them himself. The only curious feature is that Vincent had kept very quiet about it for almost ten years. Even when he was in London, he appears to have collected the illustrations of two Belgian artists, De Groux and Rops, which he gave to an English friend when he left Goupil. And, significantly, he bought a copy of the *Illustrated London News* in February 1875 for the engraved portrait of Corot that it contained. Paradoxically, during his art-dealing period in London, he preferred French artists, Belgian illustrators and French authors to anyone English. Only Millais and Boughton – as painters, however – continued to occupy him in the Amsterdam and Borinage periods. Otherwise, he was still enveloped in French and Dutch artists (Millet, Israëls and Mauve among them) and in such French periodicals as *L'Art* and *L'Illustration*. And when he eventually settled in Brussels in October 1880, he collected prints after Millet, bought two volumes of *Le Musée Universel* and took over Theo's own collection of wood-engravings, which almost certainly contained no English examples. In four successive letters written between January and April 1881 (LT 140–43) he talked of becoming an illustrator and hoped to have "a few compositions to show to Smeeton and Tilly (who ran an engraving establishment in Paris), or to the editors of *L'Illustration* or the like." (LT 143, 12 April 1881) But these same letters contain three small hints of things to come. In describing some of his own drawings, Vincent writes:

> They vaguely resemble certain drawings by Lançon, or certain English wood-engravings, but as yet they are more clumsy and awkward. (LT 140, January 1881)

It's a first glimmer: an indication that he may have been thinking of his window-gazing in the Strand. Even more encouraging is the reference that he makes in a subsequent letter:

> Many a Dutch painter would understand nothing, absolutely nothing, of the beautiful work of Boughton, Millais, Pinwell, du Maurier, Herkomer, and Walker, to name only a few artists who are real masters as draughtsmen, not to mention their talent in other directions. (LT 142, 2 April 1881)

Suddenly, there are four new names: Pinwell and Walker, du Maurier and Herkomer. Works by Pinwell and Walker, he tells us elsewhere (LT 374), he had seen for himself in London: so he is presumably remembering this, rather than naming them under the stimulus of recently renewed acquaintance. Du Maurier, on the other hand, he may well have seen in the studio of his friend Rappard, whom he had recently met in Brussels. There is a later hint of this: "I have never seen your complete collection, only the small Dürers and Holbeins and du Mauriers and some others." (R 8, 28 May 1882) But he could also have noted du Maurier's presence in leafing through volumes of *L'Art* at his uncle Cor's in Amsterdam. (LT 119, 18 February 1878) Vincent must surely have known of Herkomer's successes at the Paris International Exhibition of 1878 and the Salon of 1879. (Rappard himself had worked in Paris in the winter of 1879–80.) In brief, there is no need to suggest that he had recently seen, let alone acquired, copies of the *Graphic* – or *Punch*. Yet – and this is the third hint of a change – he gave *English* titles to two drawings he was working on just before he left Brussels in April 1881: 'The Lamp Bearers' and 'The Bearers of the Burden'.

His retreat to the parsonage at Etten from April to December 1881 temporarily interrupted his ambitions to become an illustrator. He struggled to master various media, made single figure studies of peasants, did the occasional landscape drawing, but refrained from doing any further compositions. He ceases to discuss – and collect – wood-engravings; and only twice refers to English artists (that inevitable pair, Millais and Boughton, with Herkomer's name once tagged on). Deeply wounded by the refusal of his widowed cousin, Kee Vos, to marry him, and having left Etten after a bitter quarrel with his father just after Christmas, he arrived in The Hague and took a studio of his own on the outskirts of the town. The prospects for the English illustrators could not have seemed very bright.

Herkomer   THE LAST MUSTER - SUNDAY AT THE ROYAL HOSPITAL, CHELSEA   *Graphic 15 May 1875*

Herkomer   THE BREWER'S DRAYMAN   *Graphic 20 November 1875*

C Green   THE FIREMAN   *Graphic Frontispiece Vol XX 1879*

Hopkins   THE CORNISH FISHER-LAD   *Graphic 23 June 1883*

Hopkins   HER FIRST ENGAGEMENT   *Graphic 11 November 1876*

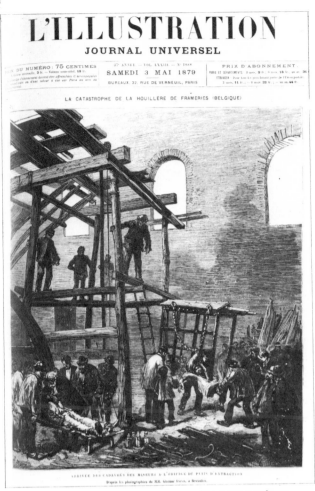

L'ILLUSTRATION
JOURNAL UNIVERSEL

PRIX DU NUMÉRO : 75 CENTIMES   27e ANNÉE — VOL. LXXIII — N° 1888   PRIX D'ABONNEMENT
SAMEDI 3 MAI 1879
BUREAUX, 22, RUE DE VERNEUIL, PARIS

LA CATASTROPHE DE LA HOUILLÈRE DE FRAMERIES (BELGIQUE)

Vierge   LA CATASTROPHE DE LA HOUILLÈRE DE FRAMIÈRES
L'Illustration 3 May 1879

Emslie   A COLLIERY EXPLOSION: VOLUNTEERS TO THE RESCUE
ILN 25 February 1882

Roll   GRÈVE DE MINEURS   *L'Illustration 29 October 1881*

Herkomer   OLD AGE – A STUDY AT THE WESTMINSTER UNION
Graphic 7 April 1877

T Green   SUNDAY AT THE FOUNDLING HOSPITAL   *ILN*
7 December 1872

Woodville   TURF-MARKET AT WESTPORT, COUNTY MAYO   *ILN*
6 March 1880

C Green   THE OUT-PATIENTS' ROOM IN UNIVERSITY COLLEGE
HOSPITAL   *Graphic 6 January 1872*

Fildes   THE BASHFUL MODEL   *Graphic 8 November 1873*

Houghton   SERVICE IN THE MORMON TABERNACLE, SALT LAKE
CITY   *Graphic 2 September 1871*

Holl   AT A RAILWAY STATION – A STUDY   *Graphic 10 February
1872*

Holl   LONDON SKETCHES: THE FOUNDLING   *Graphic 3 May 1873*

Yet shortly after settling in The Hague, he acquired his first copies of the *Graphic*, and what must have been the first pages from the *Illustrated London News* since the 'Corot' in February 1875. And from that moment in January 1882, he added to the collection whenever he could. He doesn't always disclose which volumes and years he acquired. This is especially true of the *Illustrated London News*. To define the nature and extent of his collection, some reconstruction of the stages of its growth is necessary. Otherwise, it becomes tempting to talk glibly of possible influences on Vincent's work in cases where he hadn't yet seen the illustration.

There were two main peaks of acquisition: the first in January 1882, which launched the collection, the second a year later, which gave it a remarkable comprehensiveness. The second presents few problems: he bought 21 volumes of the *Graphic* from the years 1870 to 1880, and in a sequence of letters to Rappard he enthuses about the artists, their subjects and their styles. What he acquired in the previous twelve months is less easily determined, especially as the letters that he wrote to Rappard between January and May 1882 haven't survived. However, some clues are provided in letters to Theo which enable one to establish with reasonable certainty the scope of his early purchases.

On 7 January 1882 he wrote to Theo that his first acquisitions were:

> . . . in part prints not from the cliché but from the blocks themselves . . . Drawings by Herkomer, Frank Holl, Walker, and others . . . There are things among them that are superb, for instance, 'Houseless and Homeless' by Fildes (poor people waiting in front of a free overnight shelter); and two large Herkomers and many small ones; and the 'Irish Emigrants' by Frank Holl; and the 'Old Gate' by Walker; and especially a girls' school by Frank Holl; and another large Herkomer: 'de Invaliden'.

From these clues, two main conclusions can be drawn: first, he acquired the *Graphic Portfolio* and, secondly, the main batch of *Graphics* came from issues of 1875 and 1876.

Published in 1877, the *Graphic Portfolio* was a selection of 50 "admired engravings" chosen from the early years of the *Graphic* and "printed on thick plate paper with the greatest possible care, and directly from the Original Engravings themselves, instead of from Electrotype Plates, as is of necessity the case with the usual issues of the *Graphic*; by these means the finest possible impressions have been produced." Hence, Vincent's reference to "prints not from the cliché but from the blocks themselves." These "admired engravings" were, to reverse the Ruskin thesis, a miniature Royal Academy handsomely bound in morocco. Sentimentalized genre subjects and portraits (beginning with Queen Victoria) accounted for a third of the illustrations. And the remainder reflected a reassuringly safe policy of selection. It excluded any of the strongly realistic drawings of the Franco-Prussian War and of the Commune. Equally, the London Sketches were discreetly chosen: the 'social realist' platform scarcely existed – only Fildes's 'Houseless and Hungry' and Herkomer's 'A Low Lodging-House, St. Giles's' could be called such. There was just one example of the series of the 'Heads of the People'. Many important artists – at least, later, for Vincent – were excluded: Buckman, Holl, Linton and Ridley. But there were examples by others whom he would often mention: Small (6), Green (4), Edwards (3), Gregory, Paterson and du Maurier two each. And it contained in some of the captions to the illustrations, comments on the technique of individual artists that he may have found interesting.

But he would have been more interested in the copies of the *Graphic* itself. The titles he cites in his letter to Theo all occur in issues of 1875 or 1876. (Incidentally, he repeatedly gets titles wrong in his letters – eg Fildes's 'Houseless and Hungry' becomes 'Houseless and Home-less'; or he will give them his own titles – eg 'Irish Emigrants' by Holl is actually 'Gone! Euston Station'; or he will give them descriptive titles in Dutch – eg 'een meisjesschool' by Holl is 'The School Board – Elections – A Board School', and 'de Invaliden' is clearly Herkomer's 'The Last Muster'.) From these volumes of 1875 and 1876, Vincent would have gained his first impressions of the 'Heads of the People' by Small, Herkomer and Ridley. He must also have been made aware of a few – of *the* few – 'social realist' subjects – Small's 'Festive Dinner at the Seamen's Hospital, Greenwich' and Herkomer's 'Christmas in a Workhouse'. From later references (especially from the list he gave in LT 205), it can be inferred that he took note of several Bavarian sheets by Herkomer, "scenes aboard English ships" by Gregory and Nash, Holl's 'The Deserter', a batch by W B Murray, two by Sir John Gilbert, Helen Paterson's portrait of Carlyle, and Caldecott's illustrations to *Bracebridge Hall*.

He makes no mention of further purchases in February or March 1882. But he spoke of an invitation from Blommers to show "a collection of wood-engravings after Herkomer, Frank Holl, du Maurier, etc., some evening at Pulchri . . . I have enough of them for at least two evenings." (The du Mauriers must be the pair from the *Graphic Portfolio*.) However, nothing came of this, but it enabled him to sort and arrange his collection. No purchases are recorded in April or May, yet in early June he tells Theo:

> I am getting on so well with my collection of wood-engravings, which I consider yours, I only have the use of them. I now have about a thousand sheets – English (especially Swain's), American and French ones. And Rappard, for instance, who is also collecting them now, greatly admired them; so this is something which belongs to you, though you don't know it. (LT 204, 1 or 2 June 1882)

Rappard had just visited Vincent in The Hague. From now on, the two artists shared notes on their acquisitions, exchanged duplicates, and discussed the nature and merits of wood-engraving in general. (Fortunately, Vincent's letters to Rappard have survived from May 1882 to July 1883, an indispensable addition to our knowledge of The Hague period.) This was important to Vincent. Theo had no real knowledge of the English illustrators, never collected them himself, and never sent Vincent a copy of the *Graphic* or the *Illustrated London News*.

Nonetheless, it is to Theo that Vincent sends a fairly detailed list of his collection of "about a thousand sheets". He had arranged it in 18 portfolios, classified by subject ("Irish types, miners, factories, fishers"), by artist (Barnard), or by size ("the large pages of *Graphic*, *London News*, *Harper's Weekly*, *Illustration*, etc,"); and finally, *The Graphic Portfolio*.

In July, he added Fildes's 'Empty Chair' from the Christmas Number of 1870. From a later reference to Rappard (R 24), it would seem that at this moment he bought the entire first year run (ie December 1869– December 1870), but there is some slight confusion over Vincent's use of "volume" (ie a half-year run) and "year". In September, he acquired several French periodicals, especially *L'Illustration*. By October, he had bought copies (volumes?) of the *Graphic* from 1873 and 1879, as well as some current numbers (cf references to Small, Holl and Hopkins in R 28). In November, he varied the fare by buying two old numbers of *Punch* (1855 and 1862). In December, he acquired "an old dirty torn number of 1873 from a bundle of waste paper at a bookstall". (LT 252). Yet, in the same letter, when he argues the case for the superiority of the early *Graphics* over the current ones, he uses the 'Heads of the People' as his major weapon, and this series didn't begin until 1875.

To summarize this long and rather tedious account: between January and December 1882, Vincent had *certainly* acquired the *Graphics* of 1875, 1876, 1879 and

1880, with a number of the current year's issues, and the *Graphic Portfolio*; he may *possibly* have acquired those of 1869–70 and 1873.

When, in January 1883, he bought a run of 21 volumes from 1870 to 1880, he filled the gaps at one swoop, and won himself a large number of duplicates for exchange with Rappard. He was introduced to many aspects of the work of artists he already admired (Fildes, Holl, Herkomer, Small) and made aware for the first time of the achievements of others (Boyd Houghton's drawings of the Commune and of America). But he had a problem. He wrote to Rappard:

> I am at a loss what to do. These *Graphic* series are neatly bound and in very good condition. It is almost a pity to pull them apart. But on the other hand, being able to arrange the sheets in such a way that the work of each artist is assembled is also important. (R 23, *c*20 January 1883)

He returns to the problem in his next letter to Rappard:

> If I cut out the sheets and mount them, they will show up better and I can arrange them according to the artists who did them. But then I mutilate the text, which is useful in many respects if one wants to look something up, for instance about exhibitions, although the "general surveys" of them are very superficial. And besides, one damages the novels, as eg *Quatre-vingt-treize* by Hugo. I'd also have to spend a lot on mounting board. (R 24, late January 1883)

But he overcame his scruples about dismembering the text:

> . . . I have taken the *Graphics* apart. There was a preponderant reason that made it desirable. Looking through 21 volumes is a job that takes up too much time. Of course, there is a whole lot in them that leaves me indifferent and is only useless rubbish. I think it desirable, moreover, to keep things by Small or Herkomer, or Green or Frank Holl, for instance, together, instead of having them scattered among things that do not match them in the least. When one has taken out only the best and most characteristic sheets, it is possible to get a general view of them within a few hours. And one does not need a long time to hunt up a particular thing . . . The bindings of the 21 volumes can now serve as portfolios. (R 27, mid-February 1883)

By the end of February, the operation was completed:

> I have finished cutting out and mounting the wood-engravings from the *Graphic*. Now that they are arranged in an orderly manner, they show up ever so much better. (R 29, late February 1883)

Not all of Vincent's collection has survived. The double-page engravings have all disappeared – hence, a number of them are reproduced in this catalogue to indicate something of the former extent of the collection. Some of the single-page illustrations are also lost, but many of those that remain are still mounted on the same grey paper that he used in The Hague in February 1883.

Some of these mounted sheets, however, contain examples from the *Illustrated London News*. There are three interesting points about his attitude to the *Illustrated London News*. First, that although he mentioned it only occasionally in his letters, he collected quite extensively from it. There are sheets still in the collection in Amsterdam that show something of the Irish question in 1847, 1870 and 1880; there are two splendid sheets by Gavarni from 1855, which he himself cites (R 38); there are sheets of industrial Britain (the Black Country and the industries of Sheffield, for example), that he collected from issues of the 1860's; there's Millais's 'Christmas Stories' p 74) that he got from the 1862 volume; and there's a whole sequence from the 1870's by artists as various as Fitzgerald, T Green, Macquoid, Murray and F S Walker, which shows that he collected the *Illustrated London News* as assiduously as the *Graphic*. A pattern of his acquisitions from the *Illustrated London News* can be worked out; it would be tedious to do so here. Perhaps the main difference is that he never purchased an extensive run as he did with the *Graphic*.

Secondly, there was one artist whom he wouldn't find in the *Graphic* at this period. This was Fred Barnard, who was then a frequent contributor to the *Illustrated London News*. Vincent's admiration for Barnard as the major illustrator of the Household Edition of Dickens has already been noted. It is hardly surprising that he devoted a whole portfolio to Barnard's work.

Thirdly, at a time when Vincent was disenchanted with the current issues of the *Graphic*, the work that he saw in the *Illustrated London News* continued to hold his attention. The Summer and Christmas Numbers from 1881 to 1883 received his approbation. He praised the work of Emslie and Caton Woodville, especially the latter's Irish subjects (p 72). He often bought a single issue simply for a specific drawing it contained. It was in this way that he acquired King's 'The Workman's Train' in April 1883 (p 63), and Emslie's 'At Work in a Woollen Factory' in August 1883 (p 69). In September 1884, on a visit to Utrecht from Nuenen, he bought two issues for their compositions by Holl and Thompson – his last recorded purchases.

How did Vincent respond to this vast collection? What special qualities did he find in these English illustrations? He wrote to Rappard:

> There is something stimulating and invigorating like old wine about those striking, powerful, virile drawings. (R 23, *c*20 January 1883)

And again:

> I know that you don't look upon Black and White the way most Dutchmen do . . . In many cases Black and White is a method that makes it possible to put on paper, relatively swiftly, effects that would otherwise lose something of what is called "spontaneity". I doubt whether, if the 'London Sketches' – for instance, Herkomer's 'Low Lodging House St. Giles' or Fildes's 'Casual Ward' – were to be painted, they would be quite as full of feeling and character as they are now in that unpolished Black and White. There is something virile in it – something rugged – which attracts me strongly. (R 20, 4 February 1883)

But the English achievement went further. Again, he wrote to Rappard:

> What you say about the French wood-engravings in general rather coincides with my own opinion. The English especially have found the *soul* of the wood-engravings – the original character that is just as peculiar as the character of etchings. Take Buckman's 'A London Dustyard', for instance, and the 'Harbour of Refuge' by Walker. Boetzel and Lavieille know how to do it too all the same, but Swain is the master. (R 30, *c*5 March 1883)

Vincent had clearly looked hard at the engraver, as well as the artist. He was as familiar with Boetzel's albums of the Salon and Lavieille's engravings after Millet (nos 96–99), as he was with Swain's and Dalziel's work in London. But for him, "Swain is the master."

Of the English artists themselves, the Big Three were Fildes, Herkomer and Holl. Charles Green, Small, and Boyd Houghton, Pinwell, Walker and du Maurier could occasionally reach them, but it was these three who got constant praise, whose works were most often discussed, and whose example provided Vincent with a spur.

Fildes's name is virtually synonymous with the so-called 'social realism' of the *Graphic*'s early years. Certainly, 'Houseless and Hungry' appeared in the first number of 4 December 1869; certainly, as Vincent was aware, it led to the commission for the illustrations to *Edwin Drood*. Yet Fildes was an infrequent contributor to the *Graphic* – a dozen drawings only between 1869 and 1874 – and much of his work strayed far away from a social realist context. His rise to fame was a paradigm for many English artists of the 1860's and 1870's. Provincial background (born Liverpool 1844), trained at South Kensington, full-time illustrator in the 1860's for periodicals and books, produced the occasional water-colour, took up oil painting in the early 1870's, exhibiting a pleasant genre scene at the Academy of 1872, he achieved his first real success with 'Applicants for Admission to a Casual Ward' (RA 1874), which, complete with a quotation from Forster's *Life of Dickens*, was

Small   THE CAXTON CELEBRATIONS   *Graphic 30 June 1877*

Holl   LONDON SKETCHES: THE DESERTER
Graphic 25 September 1875

Holl   ORDERED OFF   *ILN 13 September*
1884

Small   AN ENGLISH PLOUGHING MATCH   *Graphic 13 March 1875*

Thompson   THE GOOD SHEPHERD   *ILN*
9 August 1884

Walker   THE OLD GATE   *Graphic*
29 January 1876

Holl   GONE – EUSTON STATION   *Graphic*
19 February 1876

van Gogh   THE PEATERY   (F 1031) Photograph after a lost drawing of May 1883, 50 × 100 cm,

Lançon   UNE ÉQUIPE DE RAMASSEURS DE NEIGE   *La Vie Moderne 29 January 1881*

Nash   AMATEUR NAVVIES AT OXFORD — UNDERGRADUATES MAKING A ROAD AS SUGGESTED BY MR RUSKIN   *Graphic 27 June 1874*

Régamey   THE DIAMOND DIGGINGS, SOUTH AFRICA   *ILN 31 August 1872*

Buckman   A LONDON DUSTYARD   *ILN 1 March 1873*

van Gogh   GIRL IN WHITE IN THE WOODS   (F 8) Canvas 39 × 59 cm August 1882   *Otterlo, Rijksmuseum Kröller-Müller*

Macquoid   GIRL OF PONT AVEN   *ILN 30 December 1876*

INNOCENT: a Tale of Modern Life
By MRS. OLIPHANT.

Paterson   ILLUSTRATION TO "INNOCENT – A TALE OF MODERN LIFE" BY MRS OLIPHANT   *Graphic 11 January 1873*

Macquoid   REFLECTIONS   *ILN Christmas 1874*

van Gogh   L'ARLÉSIENNE   (F 541) Canvas 65 × 49 cm   *Otterlo, Rijksmuseum Kröller-Müller*

based on the *Graphic* engraving of 1869. Subsequently, he concentrated on portraits and a string of Venetian genre pictures. There were, however, two other 'social realist' pictures, 'The Widower' (RA 1876), and 'The Doctor' (RA 1891). But Vincent seems not to have been aware of Fildes's paintings when in London. He discovered him in The Hague in the pages of the *Graphic* and of *Edwin Drood*. Fildes's illustrations to the novel and his drawing of 'The Empty Chair' have already been discussed. Vincent also found impressive the illustrations to Wilkie Collins's *Miss or Mrs* (p 23) and Victor Hugo's *Quatre-vingt-treize* (p 72). But it was essentially 'Houseless and Hungry' – a title which often gave him trouble – that most moved him. He never actually says so, simply describing it as "poor people and tramps waiting in front of a free overnight shelter." But the vigour of the drawing and the 'sentiment' of the entire composition would clearly attract him, while certain figures, such as the mother and baby and the man in the top hat, must have provided points of reference for his own drawings of 'orphan men' and Sien and her baby.

It seems probable that Vincent knew little of Fildes the man. But he certainly read what he called "a kind of biography" of Herkomer, which was published in the *Graphic* of 26 October 1878. Herkomer's rise to fame was not dissimilar to Fildes's. Born in Germany in 1849, his family eventually settled in Southampton, he studied at South Kensington and concentrated his activities on the illustrated press, including the *Graphic*. He produced watercolours that were much influenced by Fred Walker, and exhibited his first painting at the Academy of 1873. But his great success came in 1875 with 'The Last Muster', a painted version of an illustration that had appeared in the *Graphic* of 1871 – again a close parallel with Fildes. There was something of the calculating opportunist about Herkomer; he was his own best publicity agent: he was mesmerist, musician and writer – and he succeeded Ruskin as Slade Professor at Oxford. 'The Last Muster' won him European fame at the Paris International Exhibition of 1878; his 'Eventide – A Scene in the Westminster Union' was much praised by Huysmans at the Salon of 1879.

In reading the "kind of biography", Vincent picked out other aspects of Herkomer's life:

> For some time he lived and painted in an empty house, or one that wasn't finished perhaps, because he couldn't pay any rent ... The biography also tells that he is *not* a man who works easily; on the contrary, ever since the beginning he has had to struggle with a kind of awkwardness, and no picture is finished without severe mental effort. (LT 263, 3 February 1883)

Some degree of vindication for Vincent's own struggles in The Hague as man and artist was implied. And he hadn't by any means abandoned the notion, first aired in Brussels in 1881, of becoming an illustrator himself. Indeed, in August 1883 he talked of going to London to see Herkomer and others to talk about this, and wished he could have Herkomer for a friend and adviser. (LT 314). His admiration for Herkomer the artist was unbounded. "He is superb," he wrote to Rappard; his work is "manly"; there is "simplicity and truth" in it; and as late as August 1885, he belonged to the ranks of "great masters of today", with Millet, Lhermitte and Breton. He based this estimate on some forty illustrations from the *Graphic*; and he virtually named them all in his letters. But three types can be distinguished. First, 'Sunday at Chelsea Hospital', a single-page engraving of 1871 (p 61) and 'The Last Muster' (p 29), a double-page spread of the two major protagonists in the painted version of 1875. The connexions with his own 'orphan men' drawings are obvious. Secondly, the 'Heads of the People': Vincent frequently referred to Herkomer's 'Heads of the People'. In fact, there are only three by Herkomer out of the series of ten: the 'Agricultural Labourer', the 'Brewer's Drayman' and the 'Coast-

guardsman'. But such was the power of his artistic personality for Vincent, that only Ridley's 'Miner' gets a fair hearing. Vincent used this series as the epitome of what he considered was the unsurpassed early style of the *Graphic* before decadence set in and the 'Types of Beauty' replaced it. He used it in reference to his own work in The Hague: for instance, the 'Fisherman in a Sou'wester' (p 79). And the idea is still active in Nuenen when he talks of painting thirty heads of peasants. (LT 383, October 1884).

Finally, three compositions of women, generally old women: 'Low Lodging House, St. Giles' and 'Christmas in the Workhouse', both single-page engravings (p 60), and 'Old Age – A Study at the Westminster Union', a double-page engraving (p 32). The latter was based on the painting, now in the Walker Art Gallery, Liverpool, that Huysmans praised in his Salon of 1879. Huysmans' praise of Herkomer's *modernité* is revealing as a reflection of his own Naturalist tenets in 1879. But it suggests more. Vincent wrote to Theo in April 1883:

> Recently I passed Israëls house – I have never been inside – the front door was open, as the servant was scrubbing the hall. I saw things hanging in the hall, and do you know what they were? The large Herkomer, 'Last Muster, Sunday at Chelsea,' and the photograph of that picture by Roll, 'Grève de Charbonniers' ... (LT 280)

Herkomer, Israëls, Roll: the place of what might be called 'second generation realism' in European art, say from 1870 to 1890, deserves consideration. The artist's exploitation of a crowd as a political entity or of a single identifiable type as bearer of sorrow or death leads to an uneasy play between realism and allegory, between social message and work of art, between technique and expression. Vincent himself was aware of the manifestations and contradictions of second generation realism; and he also partook of it himself with images as various as 'Sorrow' and 'The State Lottery'. And here the English influence, no matter how strong in the person of Herkomer (or of Fildes and Holl), was joined by German, French and Dutch influences in the persons of Liebermann and Uhde, Roll and Lhermitte, and Israëls, to name but a few.

Nonetheless, Vincent could still make strong claims for the English:

> What I appreciate in Herkomer, Fildes, Holl and the other founders of the *Graphic*, the reason why they still mean more to me than Gavarni and Daumier, and will continue to, is that while the latter seem to look on society with malice, the former – as well as men like Millet, Breton, De Groux, Israëls – chose subjects which are as true as Gavarni's or Daumier's, but have something noble and a more serious sentiment. That sentiment especially must remain, I think. An artist needn't be a clergyman or a churchwarden, but he certainly must have a warm heart for his fellow men. (LT 240, 1 November 1882)

Certainly Frank Holl provided his fair share of 'serious sentiment' for Vincent. Unlike Fildes and Herkomer, he was trained as a painter and practised as a painter; he didn't even have a watercolour period. He came later than they to the *Graphic*, first appearing in January 1872. He provided drawings for the magazine, and illustrations to Trollope's *Phineas Redux* in 1873; but many of his engravings were based on, or were related to, his paintings. Moreover, the majority of these were reproduced double-page, and are therefore now missing from the collection in Amsterdam. And it was these double-page engravings that Vincent particularly admired. He wrote to Theo of 'The Deserter':

> If you know the large drawing in the *Graphic* by Frank Holl, 'The Deserter', I should say she resembles the woman in it. (LT 194, early May 1882)

He wrote to Rappard of a composition which he always called "Irish Emigrants", but which is otherwise 'Gone! – Euston Station':

> I have something more to tell you in connexion with Holl's "Irish Emigrants". The character of the woman I wrote to you about is something like that of the principal figure of

that sheet – I mean the mother with the baby on her arm – that is, considered as a whole, without any attention to details. I could not give you a better description of her. (R 25, c9 February 1883)

In both cases he is referring to Sien, the prostitute with whom he lived in The Hague. And a mixture of 'serious sentiment' and remembered experiences of London coloured his description of 'The Foundling':

It represents some policemen in their waterproof capes who have picked up a baby exposed among the beams and planks of the Thames Embankment. Some inquisitive people are looking on, and in the background one sees the grey silhouette of the town through the mist. (R 24, late January 1883)

A committed, consistent social realist movement didn't really exist in the 1870's. It flickered now and again. But it lacked a group entity, a critical manifesto, and a single outstanding talent. Holl, at least, consistently maintained a run of realist subjects from his beginnings as an exhibitor until 1878, when he showed 'Newgate: Committed for Trial', a picture unknown to Vincent. But in the last decade of his life – he died at 43 – he turned almost exclusively to portraiture. It's improbable that any English critic compared his work with George Eliot's *Felix Holt*. Vincent saw the analogy: it makes a useful starter for any discussion of social realism in novel and picture of the 1860's and 1870's.

There were, of course, others – Green, Boyd Houghton and Small, for instance – who appealed to Vincent. But rather unexpected at first sight are his comments on du Maurier, and those he roughly classified as his followers, M E Edwards and Percy Macquoid. Du Maurier's work, as we have seen, Vincent may have known in Amsterdam in 1878, when he was looking at *L'Art*; and he must certainly have seen further examples *chez* Rappard in Brussels in 1881. So the six du Maurier drawings that he discovered in the *Graphic* would not be new to him. He also obtained a copy of the *Story of a Feather* by Douglas Jerrold, with illustrations by du Maurier, whom, he wrote, reminding us of the breadth of his interests, "is rather like Menzel, especially in some of his large compositions." (R 15, c29 October 1882). He is more specific in a later letter: he thought them "sunny and clear in the shadows." (R 23, c2 0January 1883). It's a true remark; but unexpected in the context of his social realist tendencies. But then Vincent was never narrow in his artistic allegiances. Even in the South, he could recall the merits of Meissonier.

In February 1883, Vincent wrote to Theo about his friend Rappard:

I think I see the influence of those same Englishmen in his work and intentions – though, of course, he is far from imitating them in the slightest. But, for instance, the fact that before his illness he went to make studies in the asylum for the blind is the direct practical result of his love for draughtsmen like Herkomer or Frank Holl. (LT 266, 11 February 1883)

A few months later, when he himself was involved on a composition of a row of potato diggers, which he thought "the strongest drawing I have ever made," he wrote:

. . . I adopted the manner of some English artists, without thinking of imitating them, but probably because I am attracted by the same kinds of things in nature. (LT 294, mid-June 1883)

A letter to Rappard written a day or so before this elucidates a little further:

. . . I want to tell you that I think what you say about the English black-and-white artists perfectly right and proper. I saw in your work exactly what you say. Well, I quite agree with you particularly about the bold contour. (R 37, mid-June 1883)

Yet only after naming a Millet etching, a Dürer engraving, Millet's large wood-engraving 'The Shepherdess', paintings by Baron Leys with "their characteristic, bold and vigorous drawing", De Groux, Daumier, "even Israëls, and at times Mauve and Maris too," does he finally arrive at Herkomer. It's a warning not to attribute too

much to the English influence; to remember the breadth of his references – Belgian, Dutch and French painter, illustrator and graphic artist all come into the reckoning.' Then again, one thinks of the bold contour in his first drawing of 'Sorrow' from April 1882. There, too, he talked of Millet's large wood-engraving of 'The Shepherdess':

How much can be done with one single line. Of course I don't pretend to be able to express as much as Millet in a single contour. (LT 186, mid-April 1882)

But then he adds in a postscript:

Of course I don't always draw this way, but I'm very fond of the English drawings done in this style, so no wonder I tried it for once.

In September 1882, he wrote to Rappard, announcing a firm declaration of intent:

And especially as I myself am working at trying to do things that interest me more and more – scenes in the street, the third-class waiting room, on the beach, in a hospital – my respect for those great black-and-white artists of the people, as for instance Renouard or Lançon or Doré or Morin or Gavarni or du Maurier or Ch. Keene or Howard Pyle or Hopkins or Herkomer or Frank Holl, and countless others, is forever increasing. (R 12, c12 September 1882)

Six weeks later, he asks Rappard:

Just tell me, how are your *watercolours* getting on? These last few weeks I have been working hard on mine; also types from the people. (R 15, c29 October 1882)

Among these watercolours was 'The State Lottery' (no 100). It was described at length in a letter to Theo:

You remember perhaps Moorman's State Lottery office at the beginning of Spuisstraat? I passed there on a rainy morning when a crowd of people stood waiting to get their lottery tockets. For the most part they were old women and the kind of people of whom one cannot say what they are doing or how they live, but who evidently have a great deal of drudgery and trouble and care.

Of course, superficially such a group of people who apparently take so much interest in "today's drawing" seem rather ridiculous to you and me, because neither you nor I care in the slightest for the lottery.

But that little group of people – their expression of waiting – struck me, and while I sketched it took on a larger, deeper significance for me than at first.

For it is more significant when one sees in it *the poor and money*. It is often that way with almost all groups of figures: one must sometimes think it over before one understands what it all means. The curiosity and the illusion about the lottery seem more or less childish to us – but it becomes more serious when one thinks of the contrast of misery and that kind of forlorn effort of the poor wretches to try to save themselves by buying a lottery ticket, paid for with their last pennies, which should have gone for food. However it may be, I am making a large watercolour of it. (LT 235, c1 October 1882)

This all suggests a *Graphic* or *Illustrated London News* subject. And four comparisons immediately suggest themselves: Fildes's 'Houseless and Hungry', Fitzgerald's 'Pawn-Office at Merthyr-Tydvil', Buckman's 'People Waiting for Ration Tickets in Paris' and Small's 'A Queue in Paris' (pp 59). Of these, the Small appears to be the closest in the compositional lay-out, in the strongly indicated rain, and in the presence of certain stock figures, for example, the old woman. Above all, the mood of abject hopelessness seems common to both. Yet the fact is that Vincent couldn't have known this drawing when he was working on 'The State Lottery'. It was published in the *Graphic* of 11 March 1871; that is to say, in a volume that Vincent didn't acquire until January 1882, three months after he had worked on his watercolour. And when he did, it was the one single-page illustration by Small that he picked out for special mention, simply calling it "excellent". The remaining three engravings were all known to him by October 1882. In addition, there was a double-page engraving by Caton Woodville from the *Illustrated London News* of March 1880, which was certainly in Vincent's possession when he was working on 'The State Lottery' (p 1). The subject, a distribution of relief tickets in an Irish turf-market, the effect of rain once more, and certain parallels in individual figures, all suggest comparisons with Vincent's composition.

Ultimately, however, it was his own working-processes that determined the final shape of the watercolour. He proceeded slowly: three weeks after he began, he told Theo he was still working on it (LT 237, 22 October 1882). His use of body colour is interesting; it was frowned upon by Mauve, but was much-used by English artists, especially those who drew for the wood-engraver – Herkomer, Small, Pinwell and Walker. Several of the figures in 'The State Lottery' are clearly based on Vincent's previous drawings, and even while he was working on it, he was constantly drawing from his models. A comparison of the sketch sent in his letter to Theo with the final composition shows how radically he altered some of these individual figures. Something that might appear to have been a free, spontaneous, rapid realisation of an observed moment, took him much time and trouble to complete.

Vincent's wish to become an illustrator can be seen in the series of lithographs he produced in November 1882. He planned to do about thirty,

> not too elaborate, but vigorously done . . . This would give us more prestige in the eyes of the people whom we shall need later, namely the editors of the magazines. (LT 243)

They were all to be single figures, based on his own previous drawings. They were to be his miniature *Graphic*; and from them – even if only six eventually resulted – he could make compositions later. And when he was asked by the printer's workmen if they could hang a copy of the old man from the almshouse (p 77) on their wall, Vincent wrote:

> No result of my work could please me better than that ordinary working people would hang such prints in their room or workshop. (LT 245, c16–18 November 1882)

This was the one moment in The Hague when his social conscience and artistic intentions found a consoling outlet.

The way he could utilize hints from the wood-engravings can be demonstrated again in a pair of compositions that engrossed him in May–June 1883. The influence of Lançon, Régamey, and even Nash and Buckman (p 36) still operates on his 'Peatery' (p 36) and its companion piece, 'The Sand Pit Diggers' (F 1028). The sheet by Lançon, acquired in September 1882, seems strongly to have affected the poses that he chose for some of his single-figure drawings of diggers. These were done in November 1882 (pp 76–77). They were then hoarded in portfolios and re-used in the large compositions of the following summer. The sheet by Régamey he thought a masterpiece: "it isn't striking at all at first sight, but the more you look at it the more you admire it," he wrote to Rappard in early July 1883 (R 38).

Almost seven years later in St. Rémy, it was another Régamey, the 'Convict Prison', one of a series on American prison life (p 64), that he requested Theo to send to him in order to make a painted copy. Perhaps the Régamey was never sent; or perhaps Vincent changed his mind and decided to work on the Doré print of Newgate. One of his best-known painted copies might well have been of an American prison by a French artist working for an English illustrated periodical.

Enough has perhaps been said to show something of the way that Vincent responded to the stimulus of his collection of wood-engravings. His enthusiasm for the artists of the *Graphic* was shared with people as various as Hardy, Huysmans and Hartrick. During his Dutch period – and especially during his stay in The Hague – they played a role similar to that of the Japanese Print in his Paris and Arles periods. As the Japanese Print was to Monticelli, Delacroix and Puvis de Chavannes, so the English wood-engraving was to Mauve, Israëls and Millet. Vincent looked for sources in subject and treatment, he sought out the personality of each artist, he came to know intimately the stylistic characteristics of each illustration. As he wrote to Rappard in early November 1882:

> I assure you, every time I feel a little out of sorts, I find in my collection of wood-engravings a stimulus to set to work with renewed zest. In all these fellows I see an energy, a determination and a free, healthy, cheerful spirit that animate me. (R 16)

NOTES AND BRIEF BIBLIOGRAPHY

SOME NOTES ON VINCENT IN ENGLAND (pp 7–13). The quotation from D Jerrold's text to Doré's *London: A Pilgrimage* (*1872*) is from p 102. Vincent must have been aware of Doré during his stay in London; it seems unlikely that he knew of Mayhew. The Mayhew–Doré/Jerrold–Graphic relationships deserve consideration: eg a comparison of their texts and illustrations reveals interesting variations in political and social attitudes as well as in the iconography of types, situations, and scenes chosen. Some comparison of Doré's drawings with those of the *Graphic*–and, indeed, *Illustrated London News* – artists can be drawn from Eric de Maré's admirable volume, *The London Doré Saw* (1973), which also contains a most useful bibliography. For London in the 1870's, see also Priscilla Metcalf, *Victorian London* (1972).

The Goupil stockbooks of The Hague branch of the firm, are now housed in the Netherlands Institute for Art History in The Hague. Catalogues of the first four exhibitions (1875–78) of the London gallery at 25 Bedford Street, Strand, don't exist in the library of the Victoria and Albert Museum. The title page of the fifth exhibition of 1879 is reproduced here (p 18). Two Goupil photogravures are reproduced (p 18), one from the *Galerie Photographique* series, often referred to by Vincent, the other from the smaller series, *Musée Goupil et Cie*. The place of Goupil in the London art dealing scene of the 1870's was a significant one, but the story of that belongs to a consideration of the London dealers' galleries of the late Victorian period. However, from some allusions to two London art dealers of the 1870's, both of whom Vincent knew, see Brian Gould, *Two Van Gogh Contacts: E J Van Wisselingh, art dealer: Daniel Cottier, glass painter and decorator*, London (1969); despite the title, Cottier was a very active dealer indeed, who had close business connexions with the Goupil branch in The Hague. Van Wisselingh crops up later in Vincent's life: for example, they took lunch together in The Hague in August 1883 (LT 318). I have excluded any discussion of Vincent's friendships with other art dealing colleagues in London (eg his principal at Goupil's, Obach, and Wallis of the French Gallery). And I have omitted any account of his most fascinating English friendship – that with Harry Gladwell, which began in Paris in 1875, continued in London in 1876, and was still active in Amsterdam the following year. I hope to publish an account of this in the near future.

The piecing together of the life of William Port Stokes has been made possible through the kindnesses of the Reference Librarian at Hounslow Public Library, the vicar of All Saints, Isleworth, both of whom gave me access to the Parish Registers of births, deaths and marriages; and Mr C E Busson, Borough Librarian of Ramsgate, who showed me the Rate Books from 1871 to 1876, where he himself had noted the presence of Stokes at 6 Royal Road, Ramsgate. My wife discovered the tombstone of the Stokes family in All Saints churchyard, Isleworth.

A brief biography of the Rev T Slade Jones (1829–83) is given by J H Taylor (*op cit*). A few snippets can be added: for example, Mr Jones ran a school at Twickenham in the early 1870's and therefore hadn't long been at Holme Court, Isleworth, when Vincent joined him. The nature of Mr Jones's activities at Turnham Green can also be clarified, thanks to the history of the church published in the first monthly numbers of the *Chiswick High Road Congregational Church Illustrated Monthly Magazine* (February–April 1890). This was kindly brought to my attention by Mrs Carolyn Hammond, Reference Librarian of Chiswick Public Library. The main points are: June 1873, Mr Jones began Sunday services in a building known as the 'Lecture Hall'; 12 May 1875, this hall was burnt down; 21 September 1875, the newly erected *iron* church was opened. It was this *iron* church (neither 'tin' nor 'wood', as is usually said in the literature on Van Gogh) that Vincent was familiar with, and which he drew as a tailpiece to his letter of 25 November 1876 (p 12). On 11 May 1881, the iron church was "bodily removed from the front part of the site to its present position at the side of the main building" (*op cit*, March 1890, p x). On the same day the foundation stone of a new church was laid; later renamed Gunnersbury Congregational Church, it still stands, but is no longer in use. The iron church was used as a Sunday School from 1881 until it was demolished about 1909.

VINCENT AND ENGLISH PAINTING (pp 13–20) Boughton's painting, 'The Heir' (RA 1873, no 1062), is dated 1873, and measures 42 × 72 inches. It was formerly in the collection of the Corcoran Gallery, Washington (sold at auction in New York, 24 January 1951: present whereabouts unknown). The reference to Henry James's review of the painting when it was exhibited in 1875 at the Goupil Gallery, New York, is from *The Painter's Eye*, edited by John L Sweeney, 1956, p 102. For reviews of Boughton's painting, 'God Speed! Pilgrims setting out for Canterbury; time of Chaucer' (RA 1874. no 982), see *ILN*, 16 May 1874, p 470, and the *Art Journal*, 1874, p 198. Boughton's and Abbey's illustrated tour of Holland which Vincent read in *Harper's* in July 1883 (R 38) appeared as a book shortly afterwards: *Sketching Rambles in Holland*, by George H Boughton, ARA; with illustrations by the author and Edwin A Abbey (New York, 1885). 'The Potato Gatherers', praised by Vincent as "the most beautiful of all", is illustrated on p 21: it makes an interesting comparison with Vincent's own composition of 'Potato Diggers' (F 1034), which he was currently working on.

For a discussion of Fred Walker's 'The Wayfarers' – the painted version as well as the etching – see Claude Phillips, *Frederick Walker and his Works* (1897), pp 22–23.

A point not raised in the Introduction was whether Vincent saw the Royal Academy exhibitions of 1875 and 1876. It would have been possible for him to have seen the 1875 exhibition: it opened on 1 May, and he didn't leave London until mid-May. But the Academy that included Herkomer's 'Last Muster' would surely have been recalled by him later, especially when he acquired the wood-engraving of this subject. In May 1876, he was in Ramsgate. He wrote on 12 May (LT 66): "This afternoon Mr Reid sent me a catalogue of the exhibition in London." It's not clear whether he means a catalogue of the Academy exhibition, or of the second London exhibition of Goupil, which also opened in May. In June he had two opportunities of seeing the Academy – *en route* to Welwyn, when he spent two days in London, and again in the last week of June when he went to London two or three times to try to become a missionary. That he didn't see any pictures on either occasion appears to be confirmed by his remark following his visit to Hampton Court (also in late June): "it was a pleasure to see pictures again." In other words, he hadn't seen any paintings since leaving Paris on 31 March 1876. Once he had moved to Holme Court, Isleworth in early July, he gives the impression that he was virtually confined to the house and garden throughout that month. Indeed, his first visit to London from Holme Court was not made until 17 August (see LT 73): by then, the Academy was closed.

Ironically, the first 'modern' pictures that he appears to have seen since leaving Goupil Paris in March was at

Goupil London in September (LT 75). Subsequently, he visited other dealers' galleries (eg on 7 October), and his last recorded mention of seeing a picture in London was on 18 November, again, somewhat ironically, at the house of Obach, his former Goupil boss. And a final irony: what he failed to see in London in 1875–76 he could see vicariously in The Hague in January 1882: the bulk of the first *Graphics* that he bought then consisted of the years 1875–76.

VINCENT AND THE VICTORIAN NOVEL: DICKENS AND ELIOT (pp 20–26). The suggestion that Harry Gladwell may have influenced Vincent's reading of Eliot in Paris in January–February 1876 is made very tentatively. The second suggestion, that his acquisition of the *Graphics* influenced his reading of *Middlemarch*, is based on (i) the evidence that he'd never mentioned the novel before (cf the list in LT 120); (ii) it fits in date – *Graphics* bought in January, reading *Middlemarch* in February, 1883; (iii) *Middlemarch* was published in parts in 1871–72; reviews of each part appeared in the *Graphic*. Vincent's description of the Millais–Graphic–Dickens–Fildes–Edwin Drood episode is a conflation of what he read in the *Graphic Portfolio* with what he read in Forster's *Life* in November 1882: to which he has added some dramatic embellishments – and distortions – in the telling to Theo. The *Graphic Portfolio* noted quite simply: "Mr J E Millais RA forwarded a copy (of the first number of the *Graphic* containing Fildes's 'Houseless and Hungry') to Mr Charles Dickens, who was so struck with the originality displayed in the drawing that he engaged Mr Fildes to illustrate *The Mystery of Edwin Drood*, the work he was engaged upon at the time of his death." For Dickens and his illustrators, see especially F G Kitton's book of this title (1899) and the centenary exhibition catalogue, *Charles Dickens*, Victoria and Albert Museum, 1970. Fred Barnard's *Character Sketches from Dickens* first appeared in 1879: six lithographs, portraits of Mrs Gamp, Alfred Jingle, Bill Sikes and his Dog, Little Dorrit, Sidney Carton, Pickwick. Afterwards, it was issued as photogravures, presumably the set that Vincent described (R 30).

VINCENT AND ENGLISH ILLUSTRATION (pp 27–41). The quotation from Hardy's letter of 11 April 1883 is taken from F E Hardy, *The Life of Thomas Hardy* (1933), p 206; that from Ruskin from Vol XIV, p 263, of *The Works of John Ruskin* (1903–12). The page numbers of the other references are Hartrick, p 3; Derek Hudson, *Munby*, p 354; and Huysmans, pp 221–22. For the Theo–Vincent collection, see the catalogue of the exhibition *Collectie Theo van Gogh*, Stedelijk Museum, Amsterdam, 1960. For Vincent and illustration, see Charles S. Chetham, *The Role of Vincent van Gogh's Copies in the Development of his Art* (unpublished thesis, Harvard University, 1960); Alan Bowness, *Vincent in England*, introduction to exhibition catalogue, *Vincent van Gogh*, The Arts Council, Hayward Gallery, 1968; V W van Gogh, *Vincent van Gogh on England*, Amsterdam, 1968, and introduction to exhibition catalogue, *Les Sources d'inspiration de Vincent van Gogh*, Paris, Institut Néerlandais, 1972, reprinted in the present catalogue (pp 5–6); *Van Rappard and the Art of Illustration* by Jan Laurens Siesling in *Anthon van Rappard his Life and all his Works*, Amsterdam, Vincent van Gogh Museum, 1974. For English Illustrations, see Gleeson White, *English Illustration: 'The Sixties': 1855–70*, London 1897; Forrest Reid, *Illustrators of the 'Sixties*, London 1928; Philip James, *English Book Illustration, 1800–1900*, London 1947; The Brothers Dalziel, *A Record of Fifty Years' Work, 1840–1890*, London 1901. There is very little on the *Graphic* artists of the 1870's: W L Thomas, the founder and owner, provided an autobiographical fragment in 'The Making of the *Graphic*',

The Universal Review, Vol II, no 5, 1888, pp 80–93; in the same number, Harry Quilter wrote on 'Some *Graphic* Artists', pp 94–104. There are references in L V Fildes, *Luke Fildes, RA: A Victorian Painter*, London, 1968; A M Reynolds, *The Life and Work of Frank Holl*, London, 1912; Sir Hubert von Herkomer, *The Herkomers*, London, 1910, and J Saxon Mills, *Life and Letters of Sir Hubert Herkomer*, London, 1923. For a refutation of the alleged social realist stance of the *Graphic*, see Michael Wolff and Celina Fox, *Pictures from the Magazines* in *The Victorian City*, edited by H J Dyos and Michael Wolff, London, 1973. For a brief account of the 'Development of Illustrated Journalism in England', see three articles by C N Williamson, *Magazine of Art*, 1890. I have omitted any discussion of the historical background in order to concentrate on Vincent's collection. I have also not referred to the Black-and-White Exhibitions held at the Dudley Gallery, London, from 1872 onwards. It was through reading reviews of these exhibitions in the *Graphic* that Vincent first came across Lhermitte. Some supporting evidence for establishing the pattern of Vincent's collecting habits has been excluded for want of space. The consequences of his bulk purchase of the *Graphic* in January 1883 have only been touched upon. These questions and others relating to his purchases of the *Illustrated London News*, I hope to discuss elsewhere. My emphasis on documentation and narration has meant that some interesting issues have been ignored: the problem of political commitment among European artists of the 1870's; the web of relationships that existed between English art and the Continent in that decade; the presence of Dutch artists in England (Israëls, Matthew Maris and, in the 1880's, Toorop); the contemporary European view of English art and illustration etc. For some allusions to 'second generation realism', see Linda Nochlin, *Realism*, London, 1971.

The genesis of 'The State Lottery' is typical of the majority of Vincent's watercolours of many-figured subjects, not only in The Hague, but also in Nuenen (cf F909, F951, F1038, F1113 and F1230). Vincent's nine surviving lithographs have still to be studied in terms of their technique, states, extant examples and relationship to his drawings. The culminating achievement of his Hague period was a series of large compositions, executed in mixed media, mostly of double-square format, that he worked on between May and July 1883 (F1026–1035). The photograph of 'The Peatery' (p 36), which Vincent himself arranged to have taken, is one of these regrettably lost compositions. They too deserve to be studied in some depth.

The literature on van Gogh is immense; only three works need to be singled out here. *The Complete Letters of Vincent van Gogh*, 3 Vols, New York Graphic Society, 1959 (in this catalogue, letters to Theo are abbreviated to LT, those to Rappard to R, followed by the appropriate number of the letter). Dr J Hulsker, *Van Gogh door Van Gogh*, Amsterdam, 1973 provides an indispensable framework for the sequence and dating of the letters. Finally, J-B de la Faille, *The Works of Vincent van Gogh*, London, 1970, the *catalogue raisonné* of Vincent's paintings and drawings (abbreviated to F, followed by the appropriate number). Other abbreviations used in the catalogue entries are few. *ILN = Illustrated London News;* RA = Royal Academy; VG Foundation = The Vincent van Gogh Foundation, Amsterdam. In the catalogue entries, no attempt has been made to provide potted biographies of the artists; and knighthoods, honours and bibliographical references are excluded.

CHRONOLOGY (pp 47–49). Chronologies covering Vincent's entire life exist in many publications: the emphasis here is placed on the three years in England, especially on the Isleworth stay (July–December 1876). A few minor corrections have been made to the reading of the Teachers' Meeting Minutes of Turnham Green Church as published by John H Taylor, 'Van Gogh in England', *Burlington Magazine*, September 1964, pp 419–20. These Minutes are now in the Greater London Council Record Office (Ac.64.48). Discoveries of the address of the Loyer house at 87 Hackford Road, Brixton, and of biographical details of Eugénie Loyer are due to Mr Paul Chalcroft; the drawing of the house (p 9) was discovered by Mr Ken Wilkie: see *Holland Herald*, Volume 8, Number 2, 1973, and a publication by Lambeth Libraries, *Van Gogh lived in Lambeth one hundred years ago* (1973). Confirmation that a public walk existed through Syon Park can be found in *Kelly's Directory of Middlesex* of 1873: " . . . one of the entrances to the park (through which there is a delightful public walk) being close to the church . . ."

VINCENT IN ENGLAND:
A BRIEF CHRONOLOGY, 1853–1876

1853 30 March
Vincent Willem van Gogh was born in Groot-Zundert (North Brabant), the eldest surviving child of Theodorus van Gogh (1822–1885) and Anna Cornelia Carbentus (1819–1907). His father was a pastor of the Dutch Reformed Church, holding the parishes of Groot-Zundert (1849–1871), Helvoirt (1871–1875), Etten (1875–1882) and Nuenen (1882–1885), all in Brabant. His mother was a daughter of Willem Carbentus, royal bookbinder at The Hague.

1857 1 May
Birth of Vincent's brother, Theo. The rest of the family were Anna (1855–1930), Elizabeth Huberta (1859–1936), Wilhelmien Jacoba (1862–1941) and Cornelis Vincent (1867–1900).

1864 1 October
Sent to the boarding school of J Provily at Zevenbergen; remained there until the summer of 1866.

1866 3 September
Sent to the State Secondary School King Willem II at Tilburg.

1868 March
Left the school at Tilburg and presumably spent the next fifteen months at home.

1869 30 July
Joined the Hague branch of the firm of art dealers, Goupil & Cie.

1872 July (?)
Visited the Belgian Salon at Brussels.

1873 March
Visited Amsterdam and saw the Dutch pictures destined for the Vienna International Exhibition. Told that he would shortly be transferred to London branch of Goupil.

12 to c17 May
Spent these days in Paris, visited the Salon, the Louvre, the Luxembourg, and Goupil & Cie.

c17–18 May
Arrived London from Paris.

19 May Monday
Probably began work at Goupil, 17 Southampton Street, Strand. His principal was Mr Obach. Address of first lodgings unknown – fellow boarders were three Germans.

1 June Whit Monday
Made an interesting excursion with the Germans.

9 June Sunday
Visited Box Hill with Mr Obach.

July
Visited Royal Academy.

5 August Monday
Visited Dulwich Gallery.

10 or 17 August Saturday
Went boating on the Thames with two Englishmen.

Late August
Moved to 87 Hackford Road, Brixton, where Mrs Sarah Ursula Loyer, a widow aged 51, and her daughter Eugénie (born April 1854) ran a small day school.

12 September Thursday
Saw pictures by Belgian artists in London.

Christmas
Spent happily with the Loyers.

1874 January
Wrote to Theo: "I have a delightful home, and it is a great pleasure to me to study London, the English way of life and the English people themselves."

April
Delighted with London spring blossom – lilac, hawthorn, laburnum. Sowed a little garden full of poppies, sweet peas and mignonette. Still enjoyed his walk to and from the office – it took him about three-quarters of an hour.

May?
Declared his love for Eugénie Loyer: her refusal deeply wounded him.

June
Visited the Royal Academy. Took up drawing again, but wrote that it did not amount to much.

c27 June to 15 July
Went to stay with his family in Holland – his first return home since his arrival in London. His parents found him "thin, silent, dejected – a different being." His mother wrote, "Vincent made many a nice drawing: he drew the bedroom window and the front door, all that part of the house, and also a large sketch of the houses in London which his window looks out on; it is a delightful talent which can be of great value to him."

July
Returned to London with his sister Anna, who was looking for a post as governess.

August
Left the Loyers' and took furnished rooms at 395, Kennington New Road. Ceased to draw, but read a great deal.

October
Transferred to the Goupil branch in Paris, much against his will. Remained there until Christmas.

Christmas
Spent at the parsonage at Helvoirt with his family (LT 82a).

1875 January
Returned to London and 395, Kennington New Road.

February
Visited Winter Exhibition at Burlington House. Reading Michelet, Renan, Heine and George Eliot's *Adam Bede*.

24 April
Almost certainly visited Christie's for Mendel Sale, which contained Millais's 'Chill October'.

Mid-May
Transferred to Paris branch of Goupil & Cie. Took room in Montmartre – address unknown.

June
Visited Hôtel Drouot for Gavet collection of Millet drawings.

October
Harry Gladwell, aged eighteen, son of London art dealer and apprenticed to Goupil, joined him in Montmartre. They shared breakfasts, walks, visits to galleries, prints, and Bible-reading.

Christmas
Spent at Etten with his family.

1876 January
Returned to Paris. Given three-months' notice by Goupil. Read George Eliot's *Felix Holt*.

February
Read Eliot's *Scenes of Clerical Life*.

March
Read *Kenelm Chillingly* by Bulwer-Lytton. Visited the gallery of Durand-Ruel where he bought an etching after Millet's 'Angelus'.

31 March
Left Goupil; Gladwell saw him off from Paris. Spent a happy fortnight with his parents at Etten.

14 April Good Friday
Left Etten for Ramsgate.

16 April Easter Sunday
Arrived in Ramsgate to teach at Mr Stokes's school at 6 Royal Road. Received no salary – only board and lodging. Taught elementary French and German, arithmetic, and gave dictation to 24 boys "from the London markets and streets," aged ten to 14 years old. Remained two months in Ramsgate; school then transferred to Isleworth.

12 June
Left Ramsgate to walk to London, via Canterbury and Chatham. Arrived Tuesday evening; spent two nights in London (one with Gladwell's father at Lewisham) and then walked to Welwyn to see Anna. Probably spent at least one night in Welwyn, then walked to Isleworth to join Mr Stokes.

Late June
Visited Hampton Court to see its gardens, the palace and the pictures. "It was a pleasure to see pictures again." Made two or three visits to London hoping to become a London missionary, but was refused as minimum age was 24 years old.

Early July
Left Mr Stokes's school to join another school for boys run by the Rev T Slade Jones, who was also the minister of Turnham Green Congregational Church. The School was at Holme Court, Twickenham Road, Isleworth, a fine Queen Anne house, in which Vincent had an upper room at the back of the house, overlooking a garden of acacia trees where he would often watch the sun rise.

6 August
Mr Jones and his family return from holiday; the boys arrived soon afterwards. Vincent taught them Bible history. Took a walk along the Thames – "a sky such as Ruysdael or Constable would have painted."

17 August Thursday
Left Isleworth at 11am to walk to Lewisham, arrived 5pm. Gladwell family had just returned from funeral of their daughter, aged 17 years. Returned home by train to Richmond and walked along the Thames to Isleworth; arrived home at 10.15pm.

*c*19 September
Had a surprise visit from van Iterson, a former colleague in The Hague (LT 68).

23 September Saturday
Left Isleworth at 4am; in Hyde Park at daybreak; in Kennington at 7am and "rested a little in a church where I used to go so many Sunday mornings"; visited friends in London and also Goupil gallery, where he saw the drawings van Iterson had brought from The Hague. No description of journey back to Isleworth.

Early October
Told by Mr Jones that he would teach less in the future, but would work more in his parish at Turnham Green, visiting the people etc.

2 October Monday
Spoke at the prayer meeting at the Methodist Chapel, Richmond: he went there every Monday evening.

4 October Wednesday
Took a long walk to a village an hour from Isleworth.

7 October Saturday
Asked by Mr Jones to collect the boys' fees for him in East London; *en route*, visited the picture galleries around the Strand, including the French Gallery (Mr Wallis), and the gallery of Cottier, where a Dutch friend, van Wisselingh, was employed and where he saw sketches for two church windows. Returned by bus to Turnham Green, visited a Catholic church there, then walked to Isleworth, passing through a dark park, from where he saw far away the lights of Isleworth and the church with the ivy (All Saints) and the churchyard with the weeping willows on the banks of the Thames. The park was Syon Park, through which he often walked, noting its avenues of elm trees and the swans on the stream that ran through it.

9 October Monday
Spoke again at prayer meeting at Richmond Methodist church.

13 October Friday
Gave German lessons to Mr Jones's daughters, and read them Andersen's *Snow Queen*.

5 November Sunday
Preached his first sermon in Richmond Methodist church. Sent a copy of his sermon to Theo.

6 November Monday
Again at Richmond. "I have taken such beautiful walks lately – they were such a relief after the closeness of the first months here."

12 November Sunday
Taught at Sunday School at Turnham Green. Went with Mr Jones and the boys to take tea with the sexton at Acton Green.

18 November Saturday
Asked to collect fees again for Mr Jones. Left Isleworth at 4am, Hyde Park at 6.30am, then to Whitechapel, Chancery Lane, Westminster; visited Mrs Loyer, the Obachs, and the Gladwells at Lewisham, from where he wrote to Harry Gladwell in Paris. Returned by underground.

19 November Sunday
At Turnham Green in the morning; attended a Teachers' Meeting, where it was resolved "that Mr Vincent van Gog (sic) be accepted as co-worker." In the evening Vincent

walked from Turnham Green to Richmond and then on to Petersham, where he preached in the small Methodist chapel.

4 December
Attended Teachers' Meeting at Turnham Green Church, where it was resolved "that it be optional with Teachers whether they visit their own scholars or Mr Vincent visit them". The next resolution read: "Mr Richardson proposed, Mr Stanham seconded, that Mr Vincent be supplied with all the names and addresses of the scholars in the school and that he go round to each class for particulars of those who require visiting."

*c*20 December
Returned to Etten for Christmas. It was decided that he would not return to England.

1877 5 February
Teachers' Meeting at Turnham Green: resolved "that Mr Vincent be written to be asked for his resignation, as he had left the country."

CATALOGUE

ENGLISH ARTISTS

FRED BARNARD (1846–1896)

Studied at Heatherley's and with Bonnat in Paris; exhibited RA 1866–87, mostly genre subjects: eg 'Saturday Night', a scene in Whitechapel, 1876. From 1863 to his death, one of the most prolific Victorian illustrators (a regular *ILN* man in the 1870's, hence he doesn't appear in the *Graphic*). The major contributor to the Household Edition (1871–79), his Dickens drawings were greatly admired by Vincent (see Introduction). He also collected sheets from *ILN*: a complete set of 'People I have Met' (1880), showing Barnard's breezy, fluent and sometimes slick style, still exists in the VG Foundation, as also do some sheets from the *Pictorial News* of 1883, containing illustrations to G R Sims, *How the Poor Live*.

1   VENUS AND MARS AT THE LOUVRE GALLERY, PARIS   *ILN 17 January 1880*

E BUCKMAN (1841–1930)

Frequent contributor to the early numbers of the *Graphic* (almost two dozen drawings in 1869–71) but thereafter ceased; nothing included in the *Graphic Portfolio* of 1877. Contributed some ten drawings to *ILN* in the years 1871–76. Several of these *Graphic* and *ILN* drawings are cited in letters to Rappard. Two images in particular interested Vincent: no 2, which reflected his current preoccupation with the composition of a soup-kitchen described in R28; and 'A London Dustyard', both for its subject and its technique (R15 and especially R30; and see p 36). He thought Buckman's work was "drawn especially broadly and boldly and in a whole-hearted manner." (R38)

2   PEOPLE WAITING FOR RATION TICKETS IN PARIS   *Graphic 19 November 1870*
3   A REPUBLICAN PROCESSION IN LONDON – SUNDAY MORNING *Graphic 29 April 1871*

E G DALZIEL (1849–1888)

A member of the famous family of wood-engravers. An active illustrator in periodicals and books – Household Edition of Dickens and Bunyan's *Pilgrim's Progress* (1880). Vincent refers to him once only, in a letter to Rappard (R29; about 27 February 1883): "Do you know Dalziel as a black-and-white artist? I have a public house by him – something like the one by Green – excellent." This is clearly no 5; and the Green is no 21.

4   LONDON SKETCHES – FETCHING THE SUNDAY DINNER   *Graphic 1 November 1873*
5   LONDON SKETCHES – SUNDAY AFTER 1 PM   *Graphic 10 January 1874*

J C DOLLMANN (1851–1934)

Studied at South Kensington and RA Schools. Painted genre subjects, especially domestic animals. Lived in Bedford Park. Vincent cites him once only – among a list of illustrations he is sending to Rappard (R28; end of October 1882). Compare the treatment of Dollmann's 'Opium Den' with those of Doré (no 87) and Fildes (p 24); the scene was also depicted by W B Murray (*ILN* 1 August 1874) and by Lançon in *La Vie Moderne*.

6   LONDON SKETCHES – AN OPIUM DEN AT THE EAST END   *Graphic 23 October 1880*

M E EDWARDS (1839–c1910)

Also known as Mrs Freer (1866–69) and Mrs Staples (1872–), Mary Ellen Edwards was constantly confused by Vincent with Edwin Edwards (1823–79) the well-known etcher and friend of Whistler and Fantin: he refers to her as 'Miss Edwin Edwards' from her monogram MEE. A prolific illustrator from the 1860's onwards and an early and frequent contributor to the *Graphic*. Vincent associated her, in mood, sentiment and choice of subject, with Du Maurier and Macquoid. Nos 7 and 8 are cited in R24 (end of January 1883), together with 'The Foundling' which appeared in the *Graphic* of 4 May 1878.

7   A SWIMMING CLASS AT BRIGHTON *Graphic 23 September 1871*
8   THE SPECIAL TRAIN FOR THE MEET *Graphic 23 March 1872*

A E EMSLIE (1848–1918)

Occasional contributions to *ILN* in late 1870's; appeared regularly in early 1880's. Choice of subject varied: Vincent enthuses over the drawing of a mining accident (R12; c12 September 1882 and LT 238 c10 October 1882; see p 31). He sent 'Nearing Home' from the Christmas Number of 1880 to Rappard (R28, end of October 1882). He described (R16, c31 October 1882) the acquisition of "another beautiful sheet by Emslie, 'The Rising of the Waters', a peasant woman with two children on a half-flooded meadow with pollard willows" (*ILN* 17 December 1881), which he must have partly associated with Sien and her two children. And finally, he singled out what he called "a cotton mill" (no 9) among the few wood-engravings that he had been able to acquire in the winter of 1883–84 (R40, 25 February 1884): an appropriate acquisition in relation to the series of weavers that Vincent was then working on, and also as a comparison to a composition of a 'Silversmith Workshop' that Rappard had made in 1883 and which Vincent had seen (Rappard 1974, nos 94–95).

9   AT WORK IN A WOOLLEN FACTORY *ILN 25 August 1883*

S L FILDES (1844–1927)

Fildes's early life, training, and activities as an illustrator are discussed in the Introduction. Although he helped launch the *Graphic* on 4 December 1869 with 'Houseless and Hungry', Fildes was by no means a regular contributor (from 1869 to 1874, only a dozen drawings; nothing from 1874 to 1880, when he produced weekly illustrations to the novel, *Lord Brackenbury*, by Amelia B. Edwards). For Vincent, Fildes's direct connection with Dickens as the illustrator of *Edwin Drood* and the creator of 'The Empty Chair' was crucial. Otherwise, in a letter of late January 1883 to Rappard (R24), Vincent refers to 'The Bashful Model', a double-page engraving of 8 November 1873: "Fildes has a scene in a prison yard where policemen are holding a thief or a murderer whose picture they want to take. The man won't submit to it and is struggling. In the opposite corner of the composition, the photographer and the spectators." (see p 32). In the same letter, Vincent describes "another magnificent illustration by Fildes (for a novel): two men in a churchyard in the twilight." The novel was *Miss or Mrs* by Wilkie Collins, which appeared in the Christmas Number of 1871 (see no 12).

10   HOUSELESS AND HUNGRY   *Graphic 4 December 1869*
11   ILLUSTRATION TO 'MISS OR MRS' *Graphic Christmas Number 1871*
12   ILLUSTRATION TO 'MISS OR MRS' *Graphic Christmas Number 1871*
13   "NINETY-THREE" – THE FUGITIVES IN THE FOREST OF LA SAUDRAIE *Graphic 28 February 1874*

M FITZGERALD (dates unknown)

Something of a mystery: no biographical details known. Exhibited two works at RA and others in Liverpool and Dublin between 1875 and 1885. The monogram MF perplexed Vincent: it can however be identified as M Fitzgerald from a double-page engraving in the *ILN* of 1874 and from other contributions to the *Pictorial World* of 1874–75. Fitzgerald seems not to have contributed to the *Graphic*. Vincent made two references to him: the first in R26 of c12 February 1883: "'Poor Irish Scholar' is another one by that same MF who did the 'Merthyr Tydfil Pawn Office'. However small this print may be, it's marvellously good, isn't it?" Secondly, in R38 of early July 1883, where he is describing the recent acquisition of old copies of the *ILN*: "And by MF a sheet of medium size representing the treadmill in a prison, as beautiful as a Régamey." This last reference is to Régamey's prison series (see no 93) – and Fitzgerald himself had done a series of drawings of Newgate in 1873. In Fitzgerald's work, then, Vincent found sympathetic representations of the Irish poor, the Welsh miners during a strike, and an English prison. And it seems possible that the 'Pawn Office' contributed something to the mood, composition and technique of Vincent's 'State Lottery' (see no 100).

14   SKETCHES IN THE CLERKENWELL HOUSE OF CORRECTION: THE TREADWHEEL   *ILN 4 July 1874*
15   A PAWN-OFFICE AT MERTHYR-TYDFIL   *ILN 20 February 1875*

M BIRKET FOSTER (1825–1899)

Vincent evidently knew of the characteristic rustic idylls of this prolific and highly successful watercolourist and illustrator. Writing to Rappard at the end of October 1882 (R15) Vincent confesses, "Speaking of landscapes, I've always liked Birket Foster and Read, even though they are considered old-fashioned . . . English landscape painting is very divergent in conception. Foster is very little like Edwin Edwards, but both styles have their *raison d'être*" How many works of Foster Vincent knew is problematical: he could have seen – even if he didn't own – some of the illustrated volumes. And he could have seen some in earlier numbers of the *ILN*. As far as the *Graphic* was concerned, only two examples were included in issues of the 1870's – no 16 and 'A Well at Hastings' (23 May 1874). At any rate, no 16 must have vividly reminded him of his days in London. It also makes an interesting comparison with Monet's 'Westminster' of 1871, now in the National Gallery.

16   LONDON SKETCHES – THE HOUSES OF PARLIAMENT   *Graphic 11 January 1873*

H FURNISS (1854–1925)

Comic draughtsman and prolific illustrator – a partner to Fred Barnard – Harry Furniss only briefly occupied Vincent's thoughts. He noted the monogram (R15, c29 October 1882) and in his next letter to Rappard, he wrote: "Do you know 'A Midsummer Night's Dream' by Harry Furniss, showing some people – an old man, a street urchin, a drunk – spending the night on a bench under a chestnut tree in the park? This sheet is as beautiful as the most beautiful Daumier." (R 16, c31 October 1882). Interestingly, this Furniss drawing chimes with several of Vincent's own drawings of autumn 1882 (cf F951 and F952 recto). Gladstone, the main protagonist of no 17, was one of the few English politicians who caught Vincent's eye; although he never mentions him in a letter. he nonetheless collected and mounted several engraved portraits of Gladstone.

17   A DIFFICULT POINT: A SKETCH IN THE HOUSE OF COMMONS   *ILN* *22 July 1882*

C GREEN (1840–1898)
Studied at Heatherley's and with J W Whymper, which gave him the professionalism and technique necessary to sustain a lifetime's activity as illustrator of many periodicals and several books (eg Dickens's *Old Curiosity Shop*, 1876). A regular contributor to the *Graphic* in what Vincent considered to be its vigorous early years, Green was always regarded very highly by him. More than a dozen titles from the *Graphic*, including several double-page engravings (see p 32) are cited by Vincent; and he frequently sent duplicates of Green's work to Rappard. While most of these designs are modern and Dickensian, Green also produced the occasional historical costume piece, as he often did in his exhibited paintings and watercolours. Yet Vincent admired these too: eg an artist painting a signboard in the time of Louis XVI was twice praised in letters to Rappard (R 8 and R 26).

18   LONDON STREET ACROBATS *Graphic 4 March 1871*
19   SKETCHES AT A MANCHESTER COTTON FACTORY, DINNER TIME *Graphic 26 October 1872*
20   "NINETY-THREE" – DEATH SPEAKS *Graphic 26 June 1874*
21   A SUNDAY AFTERNOON IN A GIN PALACE *Graphic 8 February 1879*

H TOWNELEY GREEN (1836–1899)
Elder brother of Charles Green; but less active as an illustrator. Vincent mentions him once – in a letter to Rappard of c2 July 1883 (R 38): "I also want to tell you that I have found an uncommonly beautiful sheet by T Green, a brother or something of C Green. It is a feast in a London foundling hospital, orphan girls of some kind sitting at the table. Oh, you'll be crazy about it. (see p 32). By the same, a smaller one besides 'A City Church Congregation', drawn as delicately, as exquisitely as 'Braemar' by our friend JMLR". And towards the end of the same letter Vincent wrote: "The T Greens are masterpieces."

22   A CITY CHURCH CONGREGATION *ILN 5 October 1872*

E J GREGORY (1850–1909)
Early friend of Herkomer in Southampton and London. Provided illustrations of the Franco-Prussian War for the *Graphic*: "and later specialized more in shipboard scenes" (R 20, 4 February 1883). One of these latter is no 23. Gregory's work of the mid 1870's, whether in drawings, watercolours or paintings, deserves a re-assessment; his *mis-en-page* is often novel and startling. His later work is less interesting. ARA 1883; RA 1898.

23   OUR ALLIES – SCENE ON BOARD SHIP AT JELLAH KOFFEE *Graphic 7 February 1874*

H HERKOMER (1849–1914)
Herkomer was clearly considered by Vincent as the most important member of the *Graphic* group of artists – see the Introduction for a full discussion. An almost complete set of the single-page engravings still exists in the VG Foundation. Oddly enough, Herkomer only produced seven double-page engravings for the *Graphic* in the 1870's: the two most important of these, at least for Vincent, are reproduced in this catalogue (pp 32–33).

24   A SKETCH AT A CONCERT GIVEN TO THE ITALIAN POOR *Graphic 18 March 1871*
25   SUNDAY AT CHELSEA HOSPITAL *Graphic 18 February 1871*
26   A WOODCARVING SCHOOL IN THE BAVARIAN ALPS *Graphic 2 December 1871*
27   LOW LODGING HOUSE, ST GILES'S *Graphic 10 February 1872*
28   SKETCHES IN THE BAVARIAN ALPS: THE SCHUHPLATTL DANCE *Graphic 22 March 1873*
29   SKETCHES IN THE BAVARIAN ALPS: A WIRTSHAUS *Graphic 13 February 1875*
30   HEADS OF THE PEOPLE II: THE AGRICULTURAL LABOURER, SUNDAY *Graphic 9 October 1875*
31   CHRISTMAS IN A WORKHOUSE *Graphic Christmas Number 1876*
32   HEADS OF THE PEOPLE: THE COASTGUARDSMAN *Graphic 20 September 1879*

FRANK HOLL (1845–1888)
Son of a well-known engraver. Francis Holl (1815–84); trained at the RA Schools; exhibited RA 1864 onwards. Essentially a painter. Late starter in the *Graphic*, first appearing in January 1872, and then regularly until 1876, after which he appeared very intermittently (twice in 1879, once in 1882, and once in 1883). Three types of illustration can be distinguished: (i) those drawn specially for the *Graphic* (some of which were later painted); (ii) those done after his own paintings; (iii) those illustrating Trollope's *Phineas Redux*, serialized from July to December 1873. Excluding these Trollope drawings, some twenty works were included in the *Graphic* between 1872 and 1883. The *ILN* reproduced two of his military subjects: 'Home Again!' (3 September 1881) and 'Ordered Off' (13 September 1884), the latter being specially bought by Vincent in Utrecht (R 46). Because most of Holl's drawings were reproduced double-page, only a handful of the single-page drawings survive in the VG Foundation. Hence, some of these lost large drawings are reproduced in this catalogue (p 32).

33   SHOEMAKING AT THE PHILANTHROPIC SOCIETY'S FARM SCHOOL AT REDHILL *Graphic 18 May 1872*
34   SKETCHES IN LONDON – A FLOWERGIRL *Graphic 22 June 1872*
35   WINTERING AT HASTINGS – A SKETCH ON THE ESPLANADE *Graphic 15 March 1873*

A HOPKINS (1848–1930)
Brother of the poet, Gerard Manley Hopkins. Studied at RA Schools. Drew for *Punch*, *Graphic*, and *ILN*. Watercolourist. Vincent singles out no 36 as "reminiscent of Percy Macquoid, if I may say so. How much character there is in it, and what a peculiar daylight tone." (R 26, c12 February 1883). And later (R 38, c2 July 1883), he refers to "Hopkins, children on the sea beach, very delicate of tone," which can be identified with 'The Paddling Season' (*ILN* 3 August 1872).

36   THE BOAT-RACE AND THE WEATHER: "OH DEAR, WHAT A DISAPPOINTMENT!" *ILN 30 March 1872*

A BOYD HOUGHTON (1836–1875)
Already a prolific illustrator in the 1860's (*Once a Week*, *Good Words*, and Dalziel's *Arabian Nights* among several books), Boyd Houghton was an early and consistent contributor to the *Graphic* until his premature death in 1875. His contributions can be divided into three types: (i) the Franco-Prussian War and the Commune; (ii) America; (iii) London and other scenes. All three were viewed with great enthusiasm by Vincent; all three are represented in this exhibition.

37   THE COMMUNE OR DEATH – WOMEN OF MONTMARTRE *Graphic 10 June 1871*
38   SHAKER EVANS *Graphic 26 August 1871*
39   A MORMON FAMILY – SALT LAKE CITY *Graphic 4 November 1871*
40   SKETCHES IN LONDON – BEFORE THE BAR *Graphic 11 May 1872*

EDWARD R KING (dates unknown)
Very little is known of this artist. Vincent mentions him once (R 34, c8 May 1883): "I bought an issue of the *London News* . . . because of a sheet by King – workmen in a carriage of the Underground Railway." This is no 41, which must have reminded Vincent of his own journey by underground when returning from a visit to the Gladwells at Lewisham on 18 November 1876 (LT 82), as well as of Doré's drawing of the Underground Railway (cited in LT 84, 21 January 1877).

41   THE WORKMAN'S TRAIN   *ILN 14 April 1883*

J D LINTON (1840–1916)
Essentially a watercolourist (President of the Royal Institute of Painters in Watercolours, 1884–99). but an occasional illustrator in the 1860's and often appeared in the early volumes of the *Graphic*. His work, with its unmistakable monogram, caught Vincent's eye once only: "Do you know J D Linton (monogram JDL)? A crowd of women (during a commune) of his is superb. Jewish synagogue, 'Tower', etc., are also very striking." A reasonable selection of his work still exists in the VG Foundation.

42   TWO VETERAN FRENCH STATESMEN – MM. THIERS AND GUIZOT *Graphic 19 October 1872*
43   LONDON SKETCHES – AT A MUSIC HALL *Graphic 5 April 1873*
44   LONDON SKETCHES – CURDS AND WHEY IN ST. JAMES'S *Graphic 14 June 1873*

J MACBETH (1847–1891)
Appeared infrequently in the *Graphic*: his brother, R W Macbeth (1848–1910), contributed more often. No 45, published in September of 1873, preceded a watercolour of the same subject (RA 1874 no 837), where slight changes were made in the composition.

45   SUNDAY EVENING IN CHELSEA HOSPITAL GARDENS *Graphic 20 September 1873*

P MACQUOID (1852–1925)
Son of the artist T R Macquoid (1820–1912); studied at Heatherley's, RA Schools and in France; began in *Graphic* and *ILN* as specialist *animalier* (mostly domestic), but soon branched out into other subjects. In four letters to Rappard, Vincent cites Macquoid. (i) In September 1882, in sending Rappard a batch of wood-engravings, he writes (R 12): "Please let me know whether you have a small figure of a woman by Percy Macquoid –

she is holding a light in her hand on the stairs of an armoury, where one sees the glint of armour. I think I have already given it to you, as well as a girl in white leaning against a tree, but if you do not have it I shall add it to another batch sometime. Macquoid is one of the most distinguished of the English illustrators." The two works mentioned are 'The Haunted Armoury' (no 47) and 'Reflections' (*ILN* Christmas 1874; see p 37). (ii) In mid-January 1883, he wrote (R 22): "I have found a girl's head by Percy Macquoid which is splendid; it is a wood-engraving *after a picture* of his." This work can be identified as 'Girl of Pont-Aven', featured on the cover of the *ILN*, 30 December 1876 (see p 37). (iii) In late January 1883, he wrote (R 24): "You know the work of Percy Macquoid, of Heilbuth, of Tissot when you see it, it seems to be the non plus ultra of elegance and mild refined feeling. In a certain sense it really is the non plus ultra." Later in the same letter he adds: "By Percy Macquoid a beautiful woman's figure, 'During The Reign of Terror'. Also little sketches, Cats, Chinese, mackerel fishing. Finally a large sheet, a corner of a studio – a lay figure that has fallen over, draperies worried by two playful dogs. There is preciosity in it, but it does not quite satisfy me; I think it somewhat high falutin' and overrefined." 'The Reign of Terror' (its published title) was *Graphic* 30 June 1877; Mackerel Fishing is no 46; and the "large sheet" was 'A Disarrangement in Blue', a double-page in *Graphic*, 13 November 1880. (iv) In February 1883, he wrote (R 26) of Hopkins' 'Boat Race' (cf no 36) as "reminiscent of Percy Macquoid." So Macquoid is much noticed in the winter of 1882–83; he's then forgotten. Yet there is evidence to suggest that Macquoid's work – in particular 'Reflections' and 'Girl of Pont-Aven' – influenced his own.

46   THE MACKEREL FISHERY – SKETCHES IN A DEVONSHIRE VILLAGE *Graphic 9 May 1874*

47   THE HAUNTED ARMOURY *Graphic Frontispiece to Vol XXII, July-December 1880*

G DU MAURIER (1834–1896)

In a letter of mid-February 1883 (R 27), Vincent wrote: "I now have seven large sheets by du Maurier – first and foremost 'Dieppe Harbour', the finest of them all – you know it – the others are 'Musical Rehearsal', 'Rival Grandpas' and 'Before Dinner' – now in the *Graphic* Portfolio – 'Battledoor and Shuttlecock', 'Sketch in the Monkey House' and 'Cricket Match'." Happily all these sheets survive in the VG Foundation; five of them are here exhibited.

48   BATTLEDOOR AND SHUTTLECOCK *Graphic 13 May 1871*

49   THE DARWINIAN THEORY – SKETCH IN THE MONKEY HOUSE OF THE ZOOLOGICAL GARDENS *Graphic 8 July 1871*

50   RIVAL GRANDPAS AND GRANDMAS *Graphic 5 August 1871*

51   MUSICAL REHEARSAL *Graphic 14 September 1871*

52   SOUVENIR DE DIEPPE *L'Art Vol 6 1876*

J E MILLAIS (1829–1896)

Vincent's high regard for Millais's paintings is discussed in the Introduction. The only wood-engraving that he mentions is the one here exhibited: "By Millais himself, a beautiful sheet, 'Christmas Stories'." (R 38, c2 July 1883). Thus, he seemed unaware of the crucial part that Millais played as an illustrator in the 1860's.

53   CHRISTMAS STORY TELLING *ILN 20 December 1862*

W B MURRAY (dates unknown)

Three artists remain obscure: Fitzgerald, King and William Bazett Murray. Murray is especially elusive; he occasionally exhibited at the RA and the Dudley Black-and-White exhibitions in the 1870's, but not later, yet his illustrations are still to be found in the *ILN* of the 1880's. As an illustrator, he began with Scottish scenes, but soon developed wider interests. He depicted scenes of London life in a less theatrical manner than Doré (nos 55 and 56). Secondly, he developed an interest in industrial subject matter (nos 54 and 58). Vincent refers to him only once – in his list of monograms (R 15) – but nonetheless collected his work (a fairly extensive selection still exists in the VG Foundation). And in two instances at least, he must have looked particularly hard – first at no 57 (compare with F 1035a and F 1660); and secondly, at no 58 (compare with some of Vincent's weavers).

54   SUGAR-MAKING AT THE COUNTER-SHIP REFINERY, BRISTOL *ILN 29 November 1873*

55   THE MORNING TOILET, SEVEN DIALS *ILN 5 September 1874*

56   LONDON LIFE: SACK MAKING BY LAMPLIGHT *Graphic 3 April 1875*

57   MARKET GARDENING – A WINTER'S JOURNEY TO COVENT GARDEN *Graphic 12 February 1876*

58   L'INDUSTRIE DU JUTE – LE TISSAGE DES NATTES EN ANGLETERRE *ILN 28 May 1881*

J PALMER (dates unknown)

Possibly synonymous with the wood-engraver W J Palmer. No 59 belongs to a series of six illustrations devoted to *The Trades of Sheffield* which appeared in the *ILN* of 6 and 20 January, and 10 March 1866. Other industrial subjects were gathered by Vincent from issues of the *ILN* of the 1860's, some of which still exist in the VG Foundation. Vincent wrote of no 59 (R 38, c2 July 1883): "By I don't know whom, a marvellous thing of the steel works in Sheffield; it is called 'The Fork Grinders'. It is in the style of Edmond Morin, that is to say, his most compact and concise style."

59   SHEFFIELD TRADES: FORK GRINDING *ILN 10 March 1866*

HELEN PATERSON (1848–1926)

With Mary Ellen Edwards, the only female artists among the English illustrators known to Vincent, although it seems doubtful that he realized that "Paterson" was a woman. His references to her are brief. In late January 1883, he wrote to Theo (LT 262): "Underneath a figure of an English woman (by Paterson) is written the name Dolorosa; that expresses it well." He is thinking of Sien's "pitiful woman's figure", her "pale face" and "sorrowful look" when he first met her. Curiously, he calls Michelle Fléchard in Hugo's *Ninety-Three* an Englishwoman. He corrects this a few days later in a letter to Rappard (R 21, c7 February 1883): "I saw a little figure by Paterson in the *Graphic*, an illustration for Hugo's *Quatre-vingt-treize* called 'Dolorosa'. It struck me because it resembles the woman at the time I found her." In a later letter (R 30, c5 March 1883) he asked Rappard: "Do you have the portrait of Carlyle – that beautiful one in the *Graphic*?" One must assume that he is referring to Helen Paterson's drawing of Carlyle (no 61), and not to the photograph of him reproduced in the *Graphic* of 30 April 1870, and again in the *Graphic Portfolio* of 1877 (p 38). Vincent was not to know that in August 1874 Helen Paterson married the poet and editor of *Fraser's Magazine*, William

Allingham, a close friend and devoted admirer of Carlyle. Moreover, during Vincent's first stay in London, it was Helen Paterson who illustrated Hardy's *Far From The Madding Crowd* in the *Cornhill Magazine*. But Vincent appears never to have read Hardy. In addition to the high regard that Vincent had for 'Dolorosa' and 'Carlyle', a third composition (p 37) has some parallels with Vincent's own painting, 'Girl in White in the Woods' (F 8; p 37).

60   "NINETY-THREE" – DOLOROSA *Graphic 13 June 1874*

61   CARLYLE IN HIS GARDEN *Graphic 15 August 1876*

G J PINWELL (1842–1875)

Yet another prolific illustrator of the 1860's – with Boyd Houghton, du Maurier, Millais and Fred Walker. But only three of his designs appeared in the *Graphic*. 'The Lost Child' (6 January 1870), 'The Sisters' (6 May 1871) and 'London Sketches: A Country Visitor' (22 February 1873). Only 'The Sisters' appears to have survived in the VG Foundation; and in any case, it is the only one of the three that Vincent wrote about in letters of late January 1883 to Theo (LT 262) and to Rappard (R 24). To Theo he wrote of "that Dolorosa expression" he had noted in Paterson's drawing (no 60) and continued about the Pinwell: "That drawing represents two women in black, in a dark room: one has just come home and is hanging her coat on the rack. The other is smelling a primrose on the table while picking up some white sewing. . . . He was such a poet that he saw the sublime in the most ordinary, commonplace things." To Rappard, he varies the analogy: the work of Macquoid, Heilbuth and Tissot is comparable to the lark, that of Pinwell and Fred Walker to the nightingale. "On a page of the *Graphic* called 'The Sisters', for instance, Pinwell draws two women in black in a dark room, a composition of the utmost simplicity, into which he has brought a serious sentiment that I can compare only with the full warble of the nightingale on a spring night."

62   THE SISTERS *Graphic 6 May 1871*

M W RIDLEY (1836–1888)

Ridley was an occasional illustrator in the 1860's. And this remained the pattern in the 1870's: less than twenty pages in the *Graphic* from 1869 to 1877 (and of these seven were published in 1871), and even fewer in the *ILN*. Vincent admired him for several reasons. First, for 'The Miner' in the 'Heads of the People' series: two copies of this survive in the VG Foundation, one of which, from the evidence of its physical condition, was clearly pinned up in his studio in the Hague. Secondly, for the series of drawings of 'Pits and Pitmen' (nos 63–67): interestingly, Vincent twice refers to their technique – they "remind one of etchings of Whistler or Seymour Haden." (R 23 and R 24). Was Vincent aware of Ridley's friendship with Whistler? And how odd, talking of friendship, that he should have cited Seymour Haden as well – the only occasions on which he does so. Thirdly, for Ridley's larger works (eg 'The Children's Ward in a Hospital', *ILN* 27 April 1872), often engraved by Swain, which show that "that old style of engraving, that elaborate, honest, unembellished drawing is by far the best." (R 17). Ridley deserves reassessment – both as painter and illustrator, as well as the *confrère* of Whistler and Fantin (an article in *Country Life*, 7 March 1974, by Valerie Gatty, gives a hopeful foretaste).

63	PITS AND PITMEN – PITMEN HEWING THE COAL *Graphic 28 January 1871*	
64	PITS AND PITMEN – THE NIGHT SHIFT *Graphic 4 February 1871*	
65	PITS AND PITMEN – MEN LEAVING THE PIT *Graphic 11 February 1871*	
66	PITS AND PITMEN – THE COAL DISTRICT *Graphic 18 February 1871*	
67	PITS AND PITMEN – COAL WHIPPING IN THE POOL *Graphic 25 February 1871*	
68	ON BOARD AN EMIGRANT SHIP – LAND HO! *Graphic 6 May 1871*	
69	HEADS OF THE PEOPLE VI: THE MINER *Graphic 15 April 1876*	

W SMALL (1843–1929)

William Small, a Scot like Macbeth and Murray, was one of the most active of late Victorian illustrators. Already fully engaged in the 1860's in book and periodical illustration, he was certainly from 1869 to 1875 the most consistent contributor to the *Graphic* of those artists whom Vincent might have called the Big Five – Fildes, Green, Herkomer, Holl and Small. From 1875 onwards, Small appears less frequently, concentrating on the occasional double-page, the Christmas Number, and illustrations to Trollope's *Marion Fay* (December 1881 – May 1882). Several contemporaries (eg Herkomer and du Maurier) refer to his technical expertise. Vincent's references are more general: "this man is amazingly clever" (R 15) and "his 'A Queue in Paris during the Siege' is excellent, and so are several of his 'London Sketches' and 'Irish Sketches'." But he reserves his highest praise for two of Small's double-page engravings (p 35): "Small has a superb drawing of 'Claxton (sic) showing specimens of his printing to the King'. It makes one think of Leys; there are many beautiful things by Small in the *Graphics*, of course, but this one and 'The Ploughing Match' are the most beautiful drawings of his I know." (R 24, late January 1883). A few weeks later, Vincent sent these two drawings to Rappard (R 31, mid-March 1883).

70	A QUEUE IN PARIS *Graphic 11 March 1871*	
71	SUNDAY AFTERNOON IN ST. GILES' – TEA AT THE WORKING MEN'S CHRISTIAN INSTITUTE *Graphic 13 January 1872*	
72	THE INTERNATIONAL FOOTBALL MATCH *Graphic 24 February 1872*	
73	LONDON SKETCHES – A NOVEMBER FOG *Graphic 9 November 1872*	
74	A FESTIVE DINNER AT THE SEAMEN'S HOSPITAL, GREENWICH *Graphic 13 February 1875*	
75	HEADS OF THE PEOPLE I: THE BRITISH ROUGH *Graphic 26 June 1875*	
76	HEADS OF THE PEOPLE III: AT COURT *Graphic 23 October 1875*	
77	HEADS OF THE PEOPLE V: THE BARRISTER *Graphic 11 December 1875*	

C J STANILAND (1838–1916)

By the mid-1870's, when Fildes, Green, Herkomer and Small had virtually withdrawn as regular contributors, the *Graphic* needed new men to join such stalwarts as Durand and Nash. Among these new men were Dollmann and Staniland. Staniland had previously done a good deal for the *ILN* (eg during the Franco-Prussian War). He now took over the "social realist" subjects. Vincent twice calls attention to this: "I think it very noble that no winter passed without the *Graphic* doing something to arouse sympathy for the poor. For example, I have a page by

Woodville representing a distribution of turf tickets in Ireland (p 32); another by Staniland called 'Help the Helpers', representing various scenes in a hospital which was short of money." (LT 240, 1 November 1882). And to Rappard (R 24, late January 1883), in speaking of Ridley's 'Pits and Pitmen', he refers to Staniland's 'The Rush to the Pit's Mouth' (which appeared in the *Graphic* of 31 January 1880). No 78, also a mining subject, is typical of Staniland's work at this period.

78	THE TWO WIDOWS *Graphic 31 July 1880*	

FRANCIS S WALKER (1848–1916)

Not to be confused with his more famous and influential namesake, Fred Walker. A frequent contributor to the early volumes of the *Graphic* (he was one of the main illustrators of the Franco-Prussian War). Vincent, however, only refers to him once. Among a batch of new finds that he reports to Rappard in mid-January 1883 (R 22) is "Walker Tip Girls (Charbonnières)." The copy exhibited is inscribed in pencil lower left below the margin, in Vincent's hand: *Tip-Terris*.

79	TIP GIRLS *ILN 27 February 1875*	

FRED WALKER (1840–1875)

Only three of Walker's works appeared in the *Graphic*, none of them specially designed by the artist himself. The first was the 'Lost Path,' published in the fourth issue, 25 December 1869, engraved by William Thomas himself, the owner of the *Graphic*; the image first appeared in *Good Words* of March 1862, and then as Walker's first exhibited painting (RA 1863); and Thomas's engraving is in fact *after* the painting. Vincent never refers to this: and indeed, it seems more than probable that he never saw it, for the simple reason that he never owned Vol 1 (December 1869–July 1870) of the *Graphic*. The two works by Walker that Vincent knew well were both engravings *after* paintings, and both were published after Walker's early death in 1875. 'The Old Gate' (RA 1869) appeared as a double-page on 29 January 1876; a detail from 'The Harbour of Refuge' (RA 1872) appeared as a single-page on 7 April 1877. These two images dominated Vincent's view of Fred Walker. He sent a duplicate of 'The Harbour of Refuge' to Rappard in February 1883: "And I often spoke to you, *amice*, about Pinwell and Walker. Well, here is a genuine Walker, first rate. Have I praised it too highly?" (R 25). Rappard having replied, Vincent writes: "Oh, I am not at all surprised to hear that you admire the sheets I sent you. Personally I cannot imagine anything more beautiful than 'Harbour of Refuge' or 'Low Lodging House' (ie by Herkomer)." (R 29, *c*27 February 1883). Vincent's deep attachment to this image of the old woman and young girl walking in the garden could well have affected the genesis – the 'sentiment' as Vincent might have called it – of his Arles painting of November 1888, 'Memory of the Garden at Etten' (F 496).

80	THE HARBOUR OF REFUGE *Graphic 7 April 1877*	

T B WIRGMAN (1848–1925)

In LT 252 (*c*11 December 1882), Vincent sent Theo in Paris a copy of the *Graphic* Christmas Number 1882. On the front page was a drawing by Wirgman, 'Some Graphic Artists', a group portrait of ten of the major contributors. Vincent wrote in pencil beneath the image, with lines pointing to Green, Herkomer, Gregory, Holl, Fildes, Small and Nash (ignoring only Durand, Hall and Woods): "retireeren

zich meer en meer als ik de jaargangen volg." He repeats this in his letter to Theo: "The *Graphic* neglects to say that many in the group of artists refuse to give their work, and withdraw more and more." The reasons for Vincent's polemic are discussed in the Introduction.

81	SOME "GRAPHIC" ARTISTS *Graphic Christmas Number 1882*	

R CATON WOODVILLE (1856–1926)

In Caton Woodville, Vincent saw the illustrator of Ireland – the Ireland of 1880 as presented in the pages of the *ILN*. He greatly admired a double-page engraving 'Turf-market at Westport, County Mayo' of 6 March 1880 (p 32): he wrote of this to Theo (LT 240) and to Rappard (R 17), praising its clear sympathy with the poor to the one, and its solid technique to the other. He collected many single-page illustrations by Woodville, as well as by Dadd, Furniss and O'Kelly; a large number of these still survive in the VG Foundation.

82	THE STATE OF IRELAND: SCENE OUTSIDE THE COURTHOUSE, GALWAY *ILN 14 February 1880*	
83	A FISHERMAN'S CABIN IN CONNEMARA *ILN 13 March 1880*	
84	THE STATE OF IRELAND: WOMEN CARRYING HOME MEAL-SACKS FROM THE RELIEF COMMITTEE *ILN 20 November 1880*	

FRENCH ARTISTS

GUSTAVE DORÉ (1832–1883)

Doré's 'London: A Pilgrimage' was published in 1872. There is no direct evidence that Vincent knew of the book during his stay in England. It also seems unlikely that he ever owned it: twice in The Hague he regrets not being able to buy it – in June 1882 (LT 204) and in September 1882 (R 13). In effect, his collection of Doré's London drawings was culled from two sources. First, the Dutch illustrated periodical, the *Katholieke Illustratie* – Vincent wrote from Dordrecht in January 1877 (LT 84): "If you can afford it – if I can, I will do the same – you must subscribe to the *Catholic Illustration* of this year; there are prints in it from London by Doré – the wharves on the Thames, Westminster, Whitechapel, the underground railway, etc." Either Theo or Vincent must have subscribed, for the vast majority of the sheets in the VG Foundation come from this source. Secondly, the French illustrated periodical, *Le Musée Universel*. In a letter from Cuesmes of 7 September 1880, Vincent told Theo: "The other day I bought for 2.50 francs two volumes of the *Musée Universel*, in which I found a large number of interesting woodcuts (sic), including three of Millet's." The two volumes he acquired were of 1875–76, since the three Millets appeared in the early issues of 1876; and in the issue of 18 December 1875, a review of L Enault's French edition of Doré's *London* contains two illustrations, one of which is 'St. Katherine's Docks' (no 85). In his other references to Doré's *London*, Vincent only once mentions a specific drawing – "that room in the night shelter for beggars" (R 13; no 86). That is to say, none of his early letters contains a reference to 'Newgate'. For a discussion of 'Newgate' and Vincent's painted copy after Doré, see the Introduction.

85	ST. KATHERINE'S DOCKS	
86	SCRIPTURE READER IN A NIGHT REFUGE	

87 OPIUM SMOKING – THE LASCAR'S
ROOM IN "EDWIN DROOD"
88 NEWGATE – EXERCISE YARD

G DURAND (1832–)

Durand was one of the mainstays of the *Graphic* from 1869 to the end of the century. Vincent himself recognized this role in his one recorded reference in which he writes of how Godefroy Durand makes current events and topics of the day to perfection (LT 252; *c*11 December 1882).

89 "NINETY-THREE" – A PARISIAN
STREET DURING THE REIGN OF
TERROR *Graphic 25 April 1874*

A-I GILBERT (1828–1899)

Gilbert – not to be confused with Sir John Gilbert – made a speciality of portraits for the illustrated press on both sides of the Channel. This portrait of Corot appeared in the *ILN* of 27 February 1875. Vincent bought the issue specially for it – indeed, he acquired a second copy, for he told Theo on 6 March 1875 (LT 23) that he was sending him "a portrait of Corot from the *London News*, which hangs in my room, too." No 90 has two sets of pinholes in all four corners and a cigarette burn top left: it could well be the same print that hung on the wall of Vincent's room in Kennington.

90 THE LATE M COROT, FRENCH PAINTER
ILN 27 February 1875

A LANÇON (1836–1887)

A frequent illustrator in the *Gazette des Beaux-Arts*, *L'Art*, *Le Musée Universel*, *L'Univers Illustré*, *L'Illustration* and *La Vie Moderne*. It was from this last periodical, founded by the publisher Georges Charpentier in 1879, that Vincent acquired this half-page drawing: it appeared in the issue of 29 January 1881. It is one of some two dozen sheets by Lançon that still survive in the VG Foundation. It is included in this exhibition as a token example of Lançon's work and as a possible source of inspiration for some of Vincent's drawings of diggers (nos 103–104).

91 UNE ÉQUIPE DE RAMASSEURS DE
NEIGE *La Vie Moderne 29 January 1881*

L LHERMITTE (1844–1925)

It was through an exhibition review in the *Graphic* that Vincent first realized the importance of Lhermitte. No 93 is part of a series of 'Les Mois Rustiques' published in *Le Monde Illustré* of 1885 and 1886.

92 LE SEMEUR *Le Monde Illustré 3 April 1886*

FÉLIX ELIE RÉGAMEY (1844–1907)

A frequent contributor to the *ILN*. Vincent appears not to have discovered him until he began buying old copies of the *ILN* in The Hague in September 1882. Régamey's American Prison Scenes (a set of four drawings published in *ILN* 19 February, 4 March, 18 March, and 17 June 1876) greatly impressed Vincent; together with Fitzgerald's series on Newgate and Renouard's series on the prisons of Paris (*L'Illustration*, 1881) they, rather than Doré's 'Newgate', formed his point of reference. Another design by Régamey that enormously impressed Vincent was 'The Diamond Diggings, South Africa' which appeared as a double-page in the *ILN* of 31 August 1872 (p 36). For its importance to Vincent's drawings – and compositions – of diggers, see Introduction.

93 AMERICAN SKETCHES: PRISON LIFE
ON BLACKWELL'S ISLAND: NO 1.
RETURNING FROM WORK *ILN 19 February 1876*

P RENOUARD (1845–1924)

An illustrator for whom Vincent had the highest regard. Many sheets still exist in the VG Foundation: he is given a token representation here. After Vincent had lost interest in the *Graphic*, Renouard became a frequent contributor.

94 LA CRISE INDUSTRIELLE À LYON:
UN CANUT À SON METIER
L'Illustration 18 October 1884

J LAURENS (after EUGÈNE DELACROIX, 1798–1863)

It was from this squared-up lithograph after Delacroix's 'The Good Samaritan' that Vincent produced his painted copy in St. Rémy (F 633).

95 LE BON SAMARITAIN
Lithograph

A LAVIEILLE (after J-F MILLET, 1814–1875)

Millet's influence on Vincent was profound and lasting. And this is well illustrated by his attitude towards, and uses of, 'Les Quatre Heures du Jour', first engraved by Lavieille in 1860. They hung in his rooms in Paris in 1875 (LT 30, 6 July 1875); he named them in Amsterdam among works that "develop a knowledge of history in general and of particular individuals from all eras" (LT 121, 3 April 1878); he copied them in Cuesmes in August 1880 (LT 134) and again in Etten in 1881 – unfortunately, none of these survives; finally, working from squared-up engravings from *L'Illustration* of 1873 (nos 96–99) he produced his four painted copies in St. Rémy in 1889–90 (F 647, 649, 684, 686).

96 LE DÉPART POUR LES CHAMPS
L'Illustration 19 April 1873
97 LA SIESTE *L'Illustration 26 July 1873*
98 LA FIN DE LA JOURNEE
L'Illustration 1 March 1873
99 LA VEILLÉE *L'Illustration 8 March 1873*

VINCENT van GOGH (1853–1890)

100 THE STATE LOTTERY
Watercolour and bodycolour,
38 × 57 cm
F 970
Described in LT 235 (*c*1 October 1882) and in subsequent letters of October 1882, this important watercolour is discussed at length in the Introduction.

101 ORPHAN MAN READING
Pencil and wash, 48 × 28.5 cm
F 966

In the same letter in which he described 'The State Lottery,' Vincent also mentioned that he was making "a watercolour of a church bench which I saw in a little church in the Geest, where the people from the workhouse go (here they call them very expressively *orphan men* and *orphan women*" (LT 235, *c*1 October 1882). And a little later in the same letter, he wrote: "Speaking about orphan *men*, I was interrupted while writing this letter by the arrival of my model. And I worked with him until dark. He wears a large old overcoat, which gives him a curiously broad figure; I think you would like this collection of old men in their Sunday and in their everyday clothes. I also drew him

sitting with a pipe. He has a queer bald head, large deaf ears and white whiskers." This same model clearly sat for both no 101 and no 102. Vincent made innumerable drawings from these "orphan men" from September to December 1882. Many have perished, like much of his Hague period work; some 40 nonetheless survive.

102 ORPHAN MAN DRINKING COFFEE
Black lithographic chalk,
42.5 × 21 cm.
SD 1682
See note to no 101. And compare the lithograph, no 108.

103 DIGGER
Pencil, 50.5 × 31.5 cm
F 906

Vincent began work on a series of drawings of diggers in November 1882. He used the "orphan men" as models. He reported in LT 243 (*c*6–8 November): "I have just finished drawing two diggers." And to Rappard (R 18, 26 November), "I drew the digger in 12 different poses and am still trying to find something better. He is a marvellously fine model, a true veteran digger." These drawings of diggers had two purposes; immediately, they could serve as guides for the series of lithographs that Vincent was working on (nos 105–110). In the long term, they supplemented his stock of drawings, carefully stored for future use in compositions. And when he eventually decided to produce a series of compositions between May and July 1883 these drawings of diggers served him to excellent purpose. Only three survive of the many he drew; nos 103 and 104, and F 907, also in the VG Foundation.

104 DIGGER
Pencil and some pen,
47.5 × 29.5 cm
F 908
See note to no 103.

105 ORPHAN MAN STANDING
Lithograph, 56 × 30 cm
Signed lower left: *Vincent*
Inscribed lower left: *Ire épreuve*
F 1658

Vincent worked on a series of lithographs – he planned to do 30 – in November 1882. Their implications for his artistic intentions, his social conscience, and his attitude towards the English illustrators are discussed in the Introduction. Here, they are simply catalogued in the order in which Vincent did them. No 105 was the first; like the rest of them, it was made from a previous drawing, which still exists (F 962)

106 SORROW
Lithograph, 39 × 29 cm
Signed lower left: *Vincent*
Inscribed lower right: *Sorrow*
F 1655

107 DIGGER
Lithograph, 52 × 37 cm
Signed lower left: *Vincent*
F 1656

108 ORPHAN MAN DRINKING COFFEE
Lithograph, 57 × 37.5 cm
Signed lower left: *Vincent*
F 1657
Compare the drawing, no 102.

109 WORN OUT
Lithograph, 49.8 × 34.6 cm
Signed lower left: *Vincent*
F 1662

110 MAN SITTING ON A BASKET CUTTING
HIS BREAD
Lithograph, 48.5 × 31.5 cm
Signed lower left: *Vincent*
F 1663

111 BUST OF A WOMAN WITH A CAP
Pencil, black lithographic chalk,
washed with white, 50 × 28.5 cm
Signed lower left: *Vincent*
F 1006

Vincent describes how he did this drawing
(LT 259, *c*11 January 1883): "To-day I
drew one (an old man's head) with lithographic crayon. Then I threw a pail of
water on the drawing, and in that moist-
ness I began to model with pencil. If it
succeeds, one gets very delicate tones; but
it is a dangerous method, which may turn
out badly. But if it succeeds, the result is
quite "non ébarbé" – delicate tones of
black which most resemble an etching. I
also did a woman's head this way, standing out against the light, so the whole is in
tone, with high lights on the profile, etc."

112 FISHERMAN IN A SOU'WESTER
Pencil, black lithographic chalk,
pen, heightened with white,
50.5 × 31.5 cm
F 1013

In a letter of *c*21 January 1883 (LT 261)
Vincent wrote: "To-morrow I get a sou'-
wester for the heads. Heads of fishermen,
old and young, that's what I have been
thinking of for a long time, and I have
made one already, then afterwards I
couldn't get a sou'wester. Now I shall have
one of my own, an old one over which many
storms and seas have passed." Almost a
month later, he wrote (LT 267, *c*15 February 1883): "I have been drawing with such
delight – fishermen's heads with that sou'-
wester I told you about; the fish scales
were still sticking to it when I got it." And
in a letter to Rappard of late January
(R 22): "What I have been working at
especially of late is heads – 'heads of the
people' – fishermen's heads with sou'-
westers, among other things." The comparison with the series of 'Heads of the
People' in the *Graphic* is therefore clear.
Several of these drawings survive: F 1010–
13, and F 1015–16, as well as No 112.

113 THE POTATO EATERS
Lithograph, 26.5 × 30.5 cm
F 1661

After the sequence of six lithographs of
figures of November 1882 (Nos 105–110),
Vincent didn't return to the medium until
July 1883. Then he produced two smaller
lithographs, 'Man Digging in the Orchard'
(F 1659) and 'Man Burning Weeds and a
Woman Sitting on a Wheelbarrow'
(F 1660). There was then a long gap until
his last experiment in the medium. 'The
Potato Eaters' was printed in April 1885;
Vincent himself was dissatisfied with the
printing. The criticisms of Rappard
eventually led to the end of their friendship. In its choice of subject, its 'sentiment', its renewed attempt to make his
art available to a wider audience, this
lithograph of 'The Potato Eaters' still
carries with it the marks of his thorough
immersion in English illustration and
literature.

HAVING BEEN FREQUENTLY [...] of *The Graphic*, so continuous and constant has been their kind information to lecturers on Art and others on the different assistance and help, for on referring to our books we find that, processes connected with the publication of *The Graphic*, besides our actual professional artists, we have no less than Two it has occurred to us that some information on the subject may Thousand Seven Hundred and Thirty good friends scattered over not be altogether uninteresting to the public. And here let us the world, constantly sending us sketches or elaborate drawings of say it is rather difficult to separate the public from the actual staff different subjects, nearly always of public interest.

SOME "GRAPHIC" ARTISTS
FROM AN ENGRAVING IN "HARPER'S MAGAZINE"

81 Wirgman SOME "GRAPHIC" ARTISTS *Graphic Christmas Number 1882*

10   Fildes   HOUSELESS AND HUNGRY   *Graphic 4 December 1869*

15   Fitzgerald   A PAWN-OFFICE AT MERTHYR-TYDFIL   *ILN 20 February 1875*

2   Buckman   PEOPLE WAITING FOR RATION TICKETS IN PARIS   *Graphic 19 November 1870*

70   Small   A QUEUE IN PARIS   *Graphic 11 March 1871*

74　Small　A FESTIVE DINNER AT THE SEAMEN'S HOSPITAL,
GREENWICH　*Graphic 13 February 1875*

71　Small　SUNDAY AFTERNOON IN ST GILES' — TEA AT THE
WORKING MEN'S CHRISTIAN INSTITUTE　*Graphic 13 January
1872*

27　Herkomer　LOW LODGING HOUSE, ST GILES'　*Graphic
10 February 1872*

31　Herkomer　CHRISTMAS IN A WORKHOUSE　*Graphic
Christmas Number 1876*

61　Paterson　CARLYLE IN HIS GARDEN　*Graphic 15 August 1876*

25 Herkomer SUNDAY AT CHELSEA HOSPITAL *Graphic 18 February 1871*

5   Dalziel   LONDON SKETCHES – SUNDAY AFTER 1 PM   *Graphic 10 January 1874*

44   Linton   LONDON SKETCHES – CURDS AND WHEY IN ST JAMES'S   *Graphic 14 June 1873*

21   C Green   A SUNDAY AFTERNOON IN A GIN PALACE   *Graphic 8 February 1879*

6   Dollmann   LONDON SKETCHES – AN OPIUM DEN AT THE EAST END   *Graphic 23 October 1880*

22　T Green　A CITY CHURCH CONGREGATION　*ILN 5 October 1872*

41　King　WORKMAN'S TRAIN　*ILN 14 April 1883*

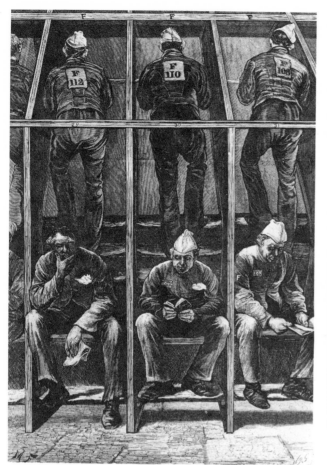

88 Doré NEWGATE – EXERCISE YARD

14 Fitzgerald SKETCHES IN THE CLERKENWELL HOUSE OF
CORRECTION: THE TREADWHEEL *ILN 4 July 1874*

93 Régamey AMERICAN SKETCHES: PRISON LIFE IN BLACKWELL'S ISLAND: NO 1 RETURNING FROM WORK *ILN 19 February 1876*

75 Small . HEADS OF THE PEOPLE I, THE BRITISH ROUGH
Graphic 26 June 1875

30 Herkomer HEADS OF THE PEOPLE II: THE AGRICULTURAL
LABOURER, SUNDAY *Graphic 9 October 1875*

69 Ridley HEADS OF THE PEOPLE VI, THE MINER *Graphic
15 April 1876*

32 Herkomer HEADS OF THE PEOPLE, THE COAST GUARDSMAN
Graphic 20 September 1879

63 Ridley PITMEN HEWING THE COAL *Graphic 28 January 1871*

64 Ridley THE NIGHT SHIFT *Graphic 4 February 1871*

79   F S Walker   TIP GIRLS   *ILN 27 February 1875*

78   Staniland   THE TWO WIDOWS   *Graphic 31 July 1880*

46 Macquoid THE MACKEREL FISHERY – SKETCHES IN A
DEVONSHIRE VILLAGE *Graphic 9 May 1874*

57 Murray MARKET GARDENING – A WINTER'S JOURNEY TO
COVENT GARDEN *Graphic 12 February 1876*

33 Holl SHOEMAKING AT THE PHILANTHROPIC SOCIETY'S FARM SCHOOL AT REDHILL *Graphic 18 May 1872*

58 Murray   L'INDUSTRIE DU JUTE – LE TISSAGE DES NATTES EN ANGLETERRE   *I LN 28 May 1881*

94 Renouard   LA CRISE INDUSTRIELLE À LYON: UN CANUT À SON METIER   *L'Illustration 18 October 1884*

9   Emslie   AT WORK IN A WOOLLEN FACTORY   *I LN 25 August 1883*

28 Herkomer SKETCHES IN THE BAVARIAN ALPS: THE
'SCHUHPLATTL DANCE' *Graphic 22 March 1873*

68 Ridley ON BOARD AN EMIGRANT SHIP – "LAND HO!"
Graphic 6 May 1871

29 Herkomer SKETCHES IN THE BAVARIAN ALPS – A
WIRTSHAUS *Graphic 13 February 1875*

89 Durand A PARISIAN STREET DURING THE REIGN OF TERROR
Graphic 25 April 1874

38 Boyd Houghton SHAKER EVANS *Graphic 26 August 1871*

20 C Green "NINETY-THREE" – DEATH SPEAKS *Graphic
26 June 1874*

Errata

The section **Vincent in England : A Brief Chronology, 1853—1876** (pp 47—49) should precede the Introduction. In the section **Notes and Brief Bibliography** (pp 43—45) the last paragraph — **Chronology** — should accordingly be brought forward.

p 14   left column, line 3 : for *Studorium* read *Studiorum*

p 19   right column, line 18 : for **spoke one** read **spoke once**

p 22   right column, half-way down : "**The sublime beginning of the** *Graphic*...." should read — "**The sublime beginning of the** *Graphic* **was something like what Dickens was as an author, what the Household Edition of his work was as a publication.**"

p 27   left column, line 19 : **Munby** should be italicised

p 28   left column, line 5 : for **Barnard** read **Bernard**

p 31   caption, upper left : for **Framières** read **Frameries**

p 34   left column, 11 lines from bottom : for **p 74** read **No 53**

p 40   right column, line 4 of long quotation : for **lottery tockets** read **lottery tickets**
        right column, last paragraph, line 6 : for **(pp 59)** read **(pp 58—59)**
        right column, last paragraph, line 15 : for **1882** read **1883**

p 43   left column, line 30 : for **However, from.....** read **However, for.....**

p 52   centre column, line 9 : for **(pp 32—33)** read **(pp 29 and 32)**
        centre column, Holl entry, last line of text : for **(p 32)** read **(pp 32 and 35)**

p 55   left column, Lhermitte entry, line 3 : for **No 93** read **No 92**

p 70   the captions to the bottom illustrations are reversed

37 Boyd Houghton THE COMMUNE OR DEATH – WOMEN OF MONTMARTRE *Graphic 10 June 1871*

13 Fildes "NINETY-THREE" – THE FUGITIVES IN THE FOREST
OF LA SAUDRAIE *Graphic 28 February 1874*

84 Woodville THE STATE OF IRELAND: WOMEN CARRYING
HOME MEAL-SACKS FROM THE RELIEF COMMITTEE *ILN*
20 November 1880

60 Paterson "NINETY-THREE" – DOLOROSA *Graphic 13 June*
1874

34 Holl SKETCHES IN LONDON – A FLOWERGIRL *Graphic*
22 June 1872

80　Fred Walker　THE HARBOUR OF REFUGE　*Graphic 7 April 1877*

62　Pinwell　THE SISTERS　*Graphic 6 May 1871*

51 du Maurier MUSICAL REHEARSAL *Graphic 14 September 1871*

48 du Maurier BATTLEDOOR AND SHUTTLECOCK *Graphic 13 May 1871*

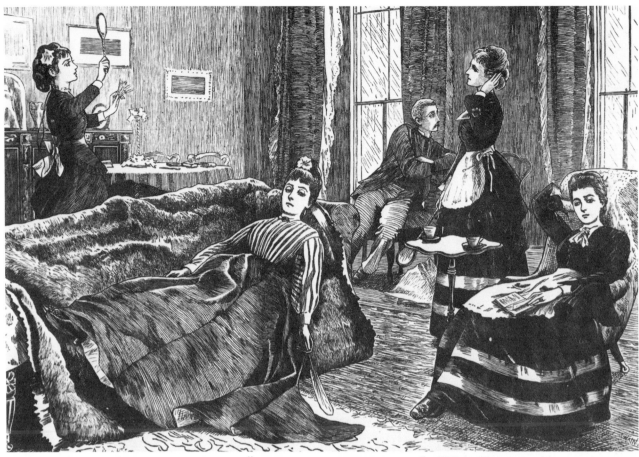

36　Hopkins　THE BOAT RACE AND THE WEATHER: "OH DEAR, WHAT A DISAPPOINTMENT!"　*ILN 30 March 1872*

8　Edwards　THE SPECIAL TRAIN FOR THE MEET　*Graphic 23 March 1872*

47　Macquoid　THE HAUNTED ARMOURY　*Graphic Frontispiece vol XXII July–December 1880*

101 van Gogh ORPHAN MAN READING (F966) Pencil and wash

102 van Gogh ORPHAN MAN DRINKING COFFEE (SD1682) Black
lithographic chalk

103 van Gogh DIGGER (F906) Pencil

104 van Gogh DIGGER (F908) Pencil
and some pen

105 van Gogh   ORPHAN MAN STANDING
(F1658) Lithograph

108 van Gogh   ORPHAN MAN DRINKING
COFFEE   (F1657) Lithograph

107 van Gogh   DIGGER   (F1656) Lithograph

106 van Gogh   SORROW   (F1655) Lithograph

109 van Gogh   WORN OUT   (F1662) Lithograph

110 van Gogh   MAN SITTING ON A BASKET, CUTTING HIS BREAD
(F1663) Lithograph

111 van Gogh BUST OF A WOMAN WITH A CAP (F1006) Pencil,
black lithographic chalk washed with white

112 van Gogh FISHERMAN IN A SOU'WESTER (F1013) Pencil,
black lithographic chalk, pen, heightened with white

113　van Gogh　THE POTATO EATERS (F1661) Lithograph